BOILED GRASS AND THE BROTH OF SHOES.

I would not be hurried
by any love of system,
by an exaggeration of instincts
to underrate the Book. We all know, that
as the human body can be
nourished on any food,
though it were boiled grass and the broth of shoes,
so the human mind can be
fed by any knowledge.
—EMERSON, *THE AMERICAN SCHOLAR.*

Quoted by Harold Bloom as the epigraph for
Figures of Capable Imagination (1976).

BOILED GRASS AND THE BROTH OF SHOES.

Reconstructing Literary Deconstruction.

RICHARD NASON.

McFarland & Company, Inc., Publishers.
Jefferson, North Carolina, and London.

British Library Cataloguing-in-Publication data are available

Library of Congress Cataloguing-in-Publication Data

Nason, Richard W.
  Boiled grass and the broth of shoes : reconstructing literary
deconstruction / [by] Richard W. Nason.
     p.   cm.
  Includes index.
  ISBN 0-89950-643-7 (lib. bdg. : 50 # alk. paper) ⊗
  1. Deconstruction. 2. Bloom, Harold. 3. Ashbery, John.
I. Title.
PN98.D43N37   1991
801′.95′09045 — dc20
                                                        91-52758
                                                        CIP

Manufactured in the United States of America.

McFarland & Company, Inc., Publishers,
  Box 611, Jefferson, North Carolina 28640.

Foreword.

(Harry Smith)

Richard Nason's *Boiled Grass and the Broth of Shoes,* as begun in 1989 in the omnibus *Pulpsmith* (volume 8) and serialized in 1990 and 1991 in *The Generalist Papers,* became a gleeful rallying point for readers and writers who detest the Deconstructionist critics and their pet poets.

While the author's artful outrage, his acrimonious wit in scourging dullards and poseurs, occasions comparison to Pope and Swift, he transcends literary criticism in his analysis of the civilized malaise, the destruction of values which has made Deconstruction possible. His thesis is that our arts have become as corrupt as our politics, as mediocre and as dull. The enthronement of Yale's Harold Bloom and Harvard's Helen Vendler in the literary establishment is seen as perfectly parallel to the rise of Yale's Bush and Harvard's Dukakis in politics. Thus Nason applies Bloom's "Map of Misreadings" to the polling place; the Deconstructionist Theme Park becomes metaphor for the national condition.

As to the fashionable Neo-Existential poets, led by "Dunce Laureate" John Ashbery, Nason exposes what he calls the "scientistic fallacy," the application of their misreadings of modern physics to human affairs, a pseudoscientific stance reminiscent of Social Darwinism in its misdirection. Though there is no lack of meaning and general predictability in quantum physics or Relativity Theory, the Neo-Existentialists make coy references to Relativity and Heisenberg's Uncertainty Principle to justify their claim for the profundity of meaninglessness and random patterns of thought.

Inevitably, of course, Richard Nason's antidote for Deconstruction has made him the founder of the Reconstruction movement.

Table of Contents.

vii

TABLE OF CONTENTS

Chapter I. Having Dislodged Eliot as the Failed Christ of Criticism, Does Harold Bloom Now See Himself as the First Coming of the Kabbalah?

I am reminded of superfluities. Here, you see, in "superfluities," I am utilizing a five-syllable word when the two-syllable "excess" might do, in order, I suppose, to demonstrate that I can clutch a complete octave of English sounds in a single fist as the first qualification to discuss the virtuosity of critic Harold Bloom, the ambitious, zealous, yea! fanatical exegete who has the court at Yale enthralled and the entire known literary world at bay in obeisance to his casuistical accomplishments. "I am reminded of superfluities" also suggests the tone of Wallace Stevens as he strums the first tentative chord in one of his interminable poetic ruminations on reality, which intrigue us as a gallicized refinement upon the Anglo-Saxon rudeness of our American poets still chopping their way through the wilderness of the American Dream (though it has been completely denuded by strip-mining), and which provide Professor Bloom, in the poetry of Stevens, with the critical link, not only to the poetry of our own past in the persons of Emerson and Whitman, but to the poetry of England as well through Stevens's connection to Keats, whom Bloom sees, erroneously I think, as a mere extension of Wordsworth and Milton.

I say "erroneously" because I sensed at the outset when first exposed to Bloom's theory of poetry as the "anxiety of influence" that the Yale professor would have a great deal of difficulty in dealing with Keats in the manner exacted by his tight little theory, that is, as essentially, merely or mainly a poet who defined himself or who could ever be defined by others in terms of his "misreading," misinterpretation or anxious reaction to earlier or "precursor" poets. This, moreover, as we shall see, fatefully turns out to be the case in the slashing and overbearing polemical thrust of the books that followed *The Anxiety of Influence: A Theory of Poetry* (1973), where Bloom attempts to cast all and sundry into the "melancholy" shade of his own influence by applying his Kabbalistic, soft, collapsible logic to the stubborn, stoic bones of the Nightingale's bard.

So to depart only for a moment longer from my own business of "superfluities," or to deal before I had planned with Bloom's "excesses" in his own terms and thereby inevitably and regrettably contribute my own to them, let me here insist that Keats did not care to waste too much time reacting to the sublime of either Wordsworth or Milton by employing any of the six "revisionary ratios" Bloom offers as the main defenses of a "strong" poet climbing anxiously to the high ground of preceding "strong" poets. And in the struggle between Keats and, not his precursor poets, but Bloom's criticism, I vehemently side with Keats's presumed contempt for Bloom's disturbance of his bones.

In any case, Keats went right over or around both Wordsworth and Milton, hugging closely to the mortal and mundane nether side of the scudding sublime, directly to the vast earthly vistas of Shakespeare where the sublime, like the starry watchmen of the night and the gilded maidens of the moon, remains at the periphery and not at the center of human experience. Keats sought out Shakespeare as the only true model for his poetic faith and the mentor for the great dramas he projected as his own true and only destiny, an expectation crushed by his early death. But Bloom cannot pursue Keats to this projected Shakespearean ground, hypothetically reclaimed by Keats for his own and succeeding generations, because it is so expansive and sensuously substantial it would overwhelm the paltry structure of Bloom's Theory with the great weight of its actuality. Bloom, as canny as a safecracker anticipating all contingencies, moves quickly to distract prospective critics from this limitation, one that he knows will deprive his Theory of the universality and the almost talismanic application that his own great ambitions demand for it.

On page 11 of the Introduction to *The Anxiety of Influence: A Theory of Poetry,* he furtively contrives this:

> The greatest poet in our language is excluded from the argument of this book for several reasons. One is necessarily historical; Shakespeare belongs to the giant age before the flood, before the anxiety of

influence became central to poetic consciousness. Another has to do with the contrast between dramatic and lyric form. As poetry has become more subjective, the shadow cast by the precursors has become more dominant. The main cause, though, is that Shakespeare's prime precursor was Marlowe, a poet very much smaller than his inheritor. Milton, with all his strength, yet had to struggle, subtly and crucially, with a major precursor in Spenser, and this struggle both formed and malformed Milton. Coleridge, ephebe of Milton and later of Wordsworth, would have been glad to find his Marlowe in Cowper (or in the much weaker Bowles), but influence cannot be willed. Shakespeare is the largest instance in the language of a phenomenon that stands outside the concern of this book. The absolute absorption of the precursor.

I have gone on perhaps too far with this quote, done to let Bloom drape the noose of his own language over the gibbet from which he will eventually be hanged, to spare myself and future decades the trouble, to illustrate the nature of his argument from anxiety and to demonstrate by its own example the monstrous and goat-like appetite of his Theory, whereby it can ingest anything it stumbles upon without a burp. Indeed, the hunger of the Kabbalah upon which it is based did not boast of three, four or seven stomachs but an infinite number. *The Anxiety of Influence,* in fact, can best be concretized by a more voracious metaphor, in its Gnostic and Kabbalistic syncretism that is, in its insidious ability to hook itself into any and all living matter and to incorporate that matter into its body, to destroy the independent life of the matter without in any way altering or inhibiting its own autonomy: It shares this capacity for destruction with cancer itself.

Beyond this, I would like to sound a warning here and now, one that should have been issued by Bloom himself, had he not been the hustling, bustling sophist that he is, but, lacking that, perhaps should be announced by the Surgeon General instead: Reading Bloom can be dangerous to your personal stability and the overall well-being of literature! *The Anxiety of Influence* (1973), by Bloom's own admission, is conceived to deal only with the poetry of the sublime. In this respect, it not only runs away from Shakespeare in fear for its life, but it also cannot tolerate about 95 percent of all the poetry ever written. It isolates finally a few major poems by a few of our poets — Milton, Blake, the Romantics — as being great enough to warrant our serious attention and in his avid pursuit of the sublime in the United States dwells obsessively upon Emerson, Whitman and Stevens. In the process, the vast majority of our greatest poets are scanted or neglected altogether simply because they do not aspire compulsively to the sublime or in so doing do not demonstrate the kind of anxiety that would make them good candidates for Bloom's eccentric Theory.

To posit anxiety over the influence of a predecessor as the controlling force for all strong poetry is to reduce the poetic impulse to a personal foible on the part of the poet not unlike the self-consciousness one might feel in the presence of a taller person on the dance floor or the intimidation common to a dark alley on a moonless night: It is the very height of absurdity. In the narrow band of sublimity where Bloom's Theory is supposed to be unexceptionable, it in no way reaches to the nature of the anxiety involved, though "anxiety" must remain Bloom's property. The word should be something closer to terror or a precarious tensing after success. It goes far beyond any Oedipal uneasiness over the imagined presence of prior great poets, to the very real threat of failure that besets any heartfelt pursuit, whether it be sex, war or art, or for that matter, a crucial ping-pong match or a hopeful entry in a flower show.

The prospect of failure presses in upon all such undertakings, whether they are measured against the prior success of others or against the practitioner's simple sense of what the art demands. Once you regard poetry as an exacting craft, which Bloom naturally enough cannot afford to do, this becomes much clearer. It is not another towering presence that intimidates the poet but his own towering expectations for his own performance. Despite what Bloom might devise in the way of an answer, these are not the same thing. That Bloom would suggest they are the same thing goes straight to the heart of the Oedipal trauma in Bloom that has driven him to develop his Theory of poetry and criticism as a kind of "defensive warfare" — and to spend thirty years of his life doing it! For indeed, any poet or other perfectionist who exhibits the kind of anxiety that Bloom attributes to his selected group of great poets would not have been fit for the enterprise. A poet may be aware of such Oedipal presences, he may even be made uneasy by their "priority." But to insist as Bloom does that this is greater than all the other biologic and cosmic forces at play within him means either that the poet or Bloom himself is in the grip of madness. The anxiety, since we still must use the word, inheres in the great risk of the enterprise and the human condition that threatens it at every turn.

We must mention the way Bloom banishes Shakespeare and disfigures Keats to underscore sharply at the outset just how Bloom's

Theory of Poetry as *The Anxiety of Influence* must finally isolate its own originator, Bloom himself, not as he sees himself, as atop the pinnacle of Everest, but as someone up a tree who can't get down. Its narrow psychological base and mania for the sublime place all narrative, didactic, bardic and ornamental poetry outside the Theory's little circle of admiration. Against the prototypes produced by his Theory, all other poetry, if it is cited at all, is mentioned only as an example of its own meanness in not attaining to the true sublime. For instance, here is Bloom on Wilde: "Oscar Wilde, who knew he had failed as a poet because he lacked strength to overcome his anxiety of influence, knew also the darker truths concerning that influence. *The Ballad of Reading Gaol* becomes an embarrassment to read, directly one recognizes that every lustre it exhibits is reflected from *The Rime of the Ancient Mariner;* and Wilde's lyrics anthologize the whole of English High Romanticism" (Introduction, *The Anxiety of Influence*). This is a fine example of Bloom's literally sophist techniques of persuasion.

Let us pause here a moment in the name of common sense, even as Bloom is reluctant to allow us to. He writes, "Oscar Wilde, who knew he had failed as a poet because he lacked the strength to overcome his anxiety of influence, knew also the darker truths concerning *that* influence." Did Wilde know "he had failed as a poet"? Did he, moreover, fail because "he lacked the strength to overcome his anxiety of influence"? And did he also know "the darker truths concerning that influence"? And if so, what were these "truths"? And why were they "darker"? Is Wilde's ballad an "embarrassment" to read? Bloom does not say *he* thinks it's an embarrassment, but that it "becomes" one, as if the mere application of his Theory inevitably causes it to undergo a mutation. And how can "one recognize that every lustre it exhibits is reflected from *The Rime of the Ancient Mariner,*" when its "lustre" is so obviously an emanation of Wilde's own readily identifiable brilliance? This quote is from the first page of *The Anxiety of Influence* and bears the ugly, graceless, ungainly sophist stamp that disfigures the 157 pages that follow.

I have no doubt that Bloom, with his frightening energy and wizard-like mental index, could find a 3 × 5 card in his file somewhere to suggest some sort of escape from the quasilibel of the dead that this sentence represents. He nonetheless knows what he would deny to those who attend his lectures, that this one declarative sentence raises a dozen questions and answers none. It is loaded with inanities and a few truly vicious imputations that are finally unverifiable. That's why Bloom runs it by us so quickly, realizing that the sense of shame still associated in the common mind with the reputation of Oscar Wilde will make reason reluctant to hold the sentence up to question. Bloom could not run a sentence like that, however, by any mind except a common one, not to mention a rather mean and sordid one at that. That's the way Roy Cohn argued. He was Senator Joseph McCarthy's legal counsel, you should recall. He made millions at such sophistry. And Bloom has been tutored well by the sophists, who argued not to clear away the encumbrances of illogic for the truth, but to make a way for themselves to absolute power over other people and the social structures wherein they moved. Bloom uses the same techniques for the same purposes, as, again, we shall see.

In that sentence Bloom rushes headlong to the point where soon he will dally interminably, as he must. For he uses the presumably vulnerable Wilde as the first buttress for his Theory of poetry as the anxiety of influence. Wilde's "failure," along with the putative "failures" of many other poets and critics of considerable grace and achievement are cast below by Bloom with great scorn, to support the premise of his Theory where the few elect will stand alone, at various stages of initiation with Milton, Goethe and Dante in the highest echelon, undoubtedly in spite of themselves. And who is finally above them all? You'll never guess. In case you are experiencing too much anxiety, let me hasten to confirm: it is none other than Bloom himself!

Like Socrates, Wilde taunted the sophists of his own day to attack him so they would in the process expose their own hypocrisy to the hard glare of history, as indeed they did. That Wilde's strategy should abide to undo a powerful sophist long after his own shame and imprisonment, in the person of Bloom, gives great testimony to the timeless nature of human integrity. Of course, Wilde today is beyond defense; he so apparently needs none; he has, sublime or not, influenced or not (and Wilde's use of "influence" you should know was lifted out of context by Bloom and twisted around in the best sophist manner to suit the warp of his Theory) his own kind of success. One that is so certain that it needs no more apology than do the form and use of a chair or a teapot or any other accepted appurtenance of our culture. *The Ballad of Reading Gaol,* though Bloom would have us shun it as an "embarrassment," persists in its resistance to both Bloom and time. As I have said, it is actuality that will overwhelm Bloom. Here are the last three stanzas of Wilde's Ballad, which is 109 stanzas long (and was written in 1896):

In Reading Gaol by Reading town
There is a pit of shame,
And in it lies a wretched man
Eaten by teeth of flame,
In a burning winding-sheet he lies,
And his grave has got no name.

And there, till Christ call forth the dead,
In silence let him lie.
No need to waste the foolish tear,
Or heave a windy sigh;
The man had killed the thing he loved,
And so he had to die.

And all men kill the thing they love,
By all let this be heard,
Some do it with a bitter look
Some with a flattering word,
The coward does it with a kiss,
The brave man with a sword!

Unwisely for Bloom but fortunately for us, the author of *The Anxiety of Influence: A Theory of Poetry* has chosen to open and close his ambitious book with little prose poems of his own. Here is the one that serves as Prologue (in its entirety), entitled "It Was a Great Marvel That They Were in the Father Without Knowing Him":

After he knew that he had fallen, outwards and
downwards, away from the Fullness, he tried to remember
what the Fullness had been.
He did remember, but found he was silent, and could
not tell the others.
He wanted to tell them that she leapt farthest forward and fell into a passion apart from his embrace.
She was in great agony, and would have been swallowed up by the sweetness, had she not reached a limit,
and stopped.
But the passion went on without her, and passed beyond the limit.
Sometimes he thought he was about to speak, but
the silence continued.

He wanted to say: "strengthless and female fruit."
We later learn that Bloom in the last provocative line is quoting Valentinus, the second-century Gnostic speculator, talking about the enticements of the Muse. Now, as Hamlet with the two pictures, one of his murdered father and the other of his murderous uncle Claudius,

8   I.   BOILED GRASS AND

face-to-face for his mother's perusal, we have the poetry of Oscar
Wilde, whom Bloom so scorns, face-to-face with the poetry of Bloom,
for your perusal. Would that we could do this for all the poets Bloom
demeans and denigrates in the name of his Theory. Judging by this
sample, it would appear that Bloom's "prime precursor" is Kahlil
Gibran, that master of pseudo–Scriptural gibberish.

This is the sort of displacement that Bloom's Theory, "a revisionary
theory of criticism," intends to bring about, subverting the strong lines
of English literature for "a deeper penetration" and "a greater severity," to give us what? Well, we see the results in Bloom's own poem
and the price it would exact in Wilde's. The Theory, as stated, is based
on little or nothing, when compared with the massive body of poetry
embraced by the very name of English verse. Based on almost
nothing, it can finally deal with almost nothing, despite the panting
conviction that Bloom attempts to breathe into the literally almost
600,000 words he has devoted to it over the last twenty-five years, as
he rose from a mere apprentice amid the bullrushes of academia to the
very heart of the hallowed grove as the nation's number one entrepreneur of criticism and the occupant of the deeply cushioned
William Clyde DeVane Professorship at Yale.

But my distaste can only prove Bloom's pleasure. Like the sophist,
he must regard all criticism of his criticism as proof of its effectiveness,
thus coupling the unchecked aggressions of the Kabbalah with the self-
promoting proclivities of the sophists, his disposition throughout his
entire later critical career (from about 1965 to 1990). Perhaps he might
be slightly, though secretly disquieted to realize there are many initiates who know exactly what he is doing; they will never be persuaded that literary history must find a new watershed in his learned
gushings; that no matter how far back he goes for the trappings of his
meagre theory, to the Greeks, the Kabbalah of the Jews or the
Gnosticism of the Christians, there are those who can lift aside "the
many veils," as he would say, and still perceive the essentially cheap
shot within the pontifical trope. Yet the effort is great, as his own many
years of industry testify; the effort is great and plagued by the persistent suspicion that either agreement or disagreement in matters he
has raised serves only to distract us from the serious business of life
and language. Still, a fool is a fool and must be followed in his fall.
Any theorist who, Faustus-like, would base an entire overview on a
fraction of a thing as if it were the whole thing, must go through the
connivances of the devil and the contortions of a carnival acrobat to

convince first himself and then the rest of the world that an almost imperceptible part can be advanced as a substitute for, indeed, an improvement upon, the bulk of the thing itself.

So does Bloom connive and contort himself as he proceeds from the
traditional critiques of *The Visionary Company* (1961) through the still
more or less conventional essays from the fifties and sixties compiled
in *The Ringers in the Tower* (1971). Now he is poised after more than
twenty years of concentrated preparation.

Before he sets forth upon his satanic leap, let us quickly sketch the
man that was, using our own equally productive (or unproductive)
revision of his revision: Influence Is Determined by Personal Circumstances. Bloom, a young student, having found the labs of the
New Criticism, full of old men poring over Eliot's flaking volumes, too
placid for his zest for upheaval, too unexplosive if you will, fervid for
power, for "priority" over the past as the same thrust that will subdue
the future, having become an automaton of the Kabbalah, Gnosticism
and Sophism through decades of strict exercise, tangled in the metaleptic and proleptic coils, bursts forth from the closet of his alchemy
with a single smoking vial of murky fluid labeled *The Anxiety of Influence,* a mere dram of which could obliterate large segments of the
literary landscape. Stand back, everyone! With *The Anxiety of Influence:
A Theory of Poetry* (1973), Bloom has arrived!

In keeping with the Faustian progression of the Kabbalah, he
moves through what he would call, after Blake's nomenclature,
"states," which are, however, described somewhat differently by the
Encyclopaedia Britannica (1911 edition): "Thus the Kabbalah encouraged
an unrestrained emotionalism, rank superstition, an unhealthy asceticism, and the employment of artificial means to induce the ecstatic
state. This brought moral laxity, a compelling reason for condemnation by the orthodoxy. . . ." Having gone around the bend in *The Anxiety of Influence* to get the sublime between his legs, Bloom plunges
from the crazed gyrations of *A Map of Misreading* (1975) and *Kabbalah
and Criticism* (1975) to the onanistic rites of *Figures of Capable Imagination*
(1976) to the seemingly maniacal reductive conclusions of *Poetry and
Repression* (1976). After this, common sense, reinforced by rumor and
numerous news reports, assures us that Bloom, author of *The Ringers
in the Tower,* has become in real life The Ringer of the Changes,
changes on his theme and Theory, changes on his ever swelling audiences throughout the country, and changes on his ever-swelling fees
at the cash register.

Prior to his narcotization by *The Anxiety of Influence,* Bloom could turn to good effect his scholarly apparatus and critical acuity to the accepted tasks of criticism. In scores of critical pieces in the fifties and sixties, he could only be regarded as a benign influence, addressing himself and leading his readers to refreshed sources showing anew how history, philosophy and literature are washed by the same waters. He performed great service within the traditional role of criticism by bringing over Nietzsche and Freud more thoroughly and profoundly than they had been before and by reintroducing Vico and a score of other authorities with new emphasis. He rectified many other oversights that the New Criticism had committed. *The Visionary Company* (1961) is nothing less than a *tour de force* of synthesis, calling on several new disciplines to revivify the impact of the Great English Romantics. It is full of brightness. In the Introduction to *The Ringers in the Tower* (1971), he seems truly concerned with the spiritual well-being of language and its practitioners. He is generous in sharing with others the hard lessons he has learned. Would only that he had hewed to his own admonitions:

> All rationalisms, from Greek to Late Victorian, fail in turn, as do all Romanticisms, for less than all cannot satisfy man. The Freudian rationalism, wisely refusing heroic failure, insists that less than all had better content man, for there can be no satisfaction in satisfaction anyway. Though this is wisdom, it can be found in only a few modern poets who do not darken it with extrapoetic persuasions, in the manner of Eliot and his followers. I can think only of Hardy and of Stevens as modern poets who divine by invention, without phantasmagoria or doctrine, without the cup of Circe or the cup of communion. If our current poets are to help us in an increasingly bad time, if they are to make the dark grow luminous, the void fruitful, they had best be found by the right precursors among the ringers in the tower of Romantic tradition.

Alas! This was written in 1969. Only a few years would pass before Bloom hastily buried his own light and grasped desperately, beyond the cups of both Circe and communion, to the cup of the Kabbalah, fuming at the brim with the "extrapoetic persuasions," "the phantasmagoria" and the "doctrine" that Bloom had seen as the death of poetry. In *The Anxiety of Influence,* he himself provides his own version of the shroud:

> All criticisms that call themselves primary vacillate between tautology—in which the poem is and means itself—and reduction—in which the poem means something that is not itself a poem. Anti-

thetical criticism must begin by denying both tautology and reduction, a denial best delivered by the assertion that the meaning of a
poem can only be a poem, but *another poem — a poem not itself.* And not
a poem chosen with total arbitrariness, but any central poem by an
indubitable precursor, even if the ephebe *never read* that poem. Source
study is wholly irrelevant here; we are dealing with primal words, but
antithetical meanings, and an ephebe's best misinterpretations may
well be of poems he has never read.

If Bloom is serious here, he may be leading his students down a path
of irrelevancies to the point of no return. If not, then like the boy who
cried "wolf," he may be haunted by his jest. And like the fellow who
shouted "fire!" when there was no fire, because the movie was boring,
Bloom may finally learn that his colleagues find his sense of humor
leaves something to be desired.

But revising Bloom's revisions, I have said: Circumstances Determine Influence. With this in mind, remember that by 1970 Bloom had
written book after book and still found himself unelected amongst the
lazy dons who droned and dozed in academia. He had to do something
to set himself apart. He had to prod them where they lived. He had
to threaten the basis for their livelihood: criticism itself. As Ben Gunn
tells Jim in *Treasure Island,* "You goes up to the Squire and you nips
him, like this!" (paraphrase). To demonstrate, Ben Gunn "nips" Jim's
cheek. Bloom nipped the professors in a much more critical part of
their collective anatomy. *The Anxiety of Influence* was the pincers he
used. But remember, Circumstances Determine Influence: Bloom
was approaching middle-age; to a man at such a juncture, the crotch
of the bitch Fame has an otherwise unaccountable allure.

Poetry and criticism are in Bloom's view a kind of warfare. He says
it many times in many different ways but never so emphatically as at
the end of *Kabbalah and Criticism* (1975):

> A poem is either weak and forgettable, or else strong and so
> memorable. Strength here means the strength of imposition. A poet
> is strong because poets following must work to evade him. A critic is
> strong if his readings similarly provoke other readings. What allies the
> strong poet and the strong critic is that there is a necessary element
> in their respective misreadings. . . . Nothing is gained by continuing
> to idealize reading, as though reading were not an art of defensive
> warfare [pages 125–6].

Perceiving criticism as warfare, Bloom would become Mars himself.
Striding within Bloom's belligerent metaphor and utilizing the
Kabbalistic prerogative to bend all language to personal advantage,

I might suggest that *The Anxiety of Influence* was Bloom's *Mein Kampf.*
Once it went forth without bringing the authorities down on his head,
as it surely should have and he suspected it might, Bloom knew the
whole literary world was soft for conquest. He would topple all around
him, not as a strident interloper but as a figure of the Establishment,
from within, and using pedantry's accepted forms of challenge and exchange. So that others might know his battle plan and techniques of
combat and join him against the foe of "classical" or standard
criticism, he promulgated a *Map of Misreading* (1975):

> ... a voyage back to literary origins is made, in quest of a map of
> misreading. From the intimate alliance between poetic origins and
> poetic final phrases, the voyage goes back first to the process of how
> literary tradition is formed, next to the sources of that process in a
> Primal Scene of Instruction [the German warrior initiation of *com-
> itas*?], and finally to a meditation on belatedness. This meditation
> centers on influence as a six-fold, defensive trope for the act of
> reading/misreading. The relation of tropes, defenses, images and
> revisionary ratios is then worked out in a chapter that accompanies
> the map of misprision....

And lest his colleagues cry they had not been forewarned even as
they are overwhelmed by a "stronger" doctrine, Bloom tossed off *Kabbalah and Criticism* for good measure, to spell out in no uncertain terms
the exotic, Eastern, unorthodox routes of his faith (like Hitler's
Aryanism?). And to support his advance should the elitists rouse
themselves from their complacencies, he called upon the common
masses in flattering terms:

> The Lurianic story of creation now seems to me the best paradigm
> available for a study of the way poets war against one another in the
> strife of Eternity that is poetic influence. Luria's story ... has three
> main stages.... The first two stages can be approximated in many of
> the theorists of deconstruction, from Nietzsche and Freud to all our
> contemporary interpretors who make of the reading subject either
> what Nietzsche cheerfully called "at most a rendezvous of persons," or
> what I would call a new mythic being—clearly implied by Paul de
> Man in particular—the reader as Overman [the German Superman
> in a Yalie blazer?], the *Überleser.*

Bloom's Master Plan had two parts, but not necessarily two phases.
They could be mutually intergenerating (this is the way Bloom writes,
to lend impact to his argument through the sheer weight of syllables):
He wanted to dominate criticism and he wanted criticism to dominate
poetry. In order to appear as the savior of criticism whose efforts at

revitalization precluded any leadership but his own, he had to present himself as a forceful innovator with a new and important message. This he did with *The Anxiety of Influence*. As he subdued the ranks of the critics, he worked to make criticism primary, or superior to poetry. By definition, critics have always agreed they were secondary to the poetic artifacts that provoked their response. Through the Kabbalah, where the interpretation could absorb the text if it were strong enough, Bloom could change all that. He could make poetry secondary to criticism. By making criticism primary, he could give even potentially antagonistic colleagues within academia new power and thus render them his loyal legions. But we must first get on an equal footing with the thing we would overturn. First, he had to make poetry and criticism coequal. To do this, through the Kabbalah, he made them interchangeable, or in essence the same thing. Thus he begins the Introduction of *A Map of Misreading:*

> This book offers instruction in the practical criticism of poetry, in how to read a poem, on the basis of the theory of poetry set forth in my earlier book, *The Anxiety of Influence*. Reading, as my title indicates, is a belated and all-but-impossible act, and strong is always a misreading. Literary meaning tends to become more undetermined even as literary language becomes more over-determined. Criticism may not always be an act of judging, but it is always an act of deciding, and what it tries to decide is meaning.
>
> Like my earlier book, *A Map of Misreading* studies poetic influence, by which I continue *not* to mean the passing-on of images and ideas from earlier to late poets. Influence, as I conceive it, means that there are *no* texts, but only relationships *between* texts. These relationships depend upon a critical act, a misreading or misprision, that one poet performs upon another and that does not differ in kind from the necessary critical acts performed by every strong reader upon every text he encounters. The influence-relation governs reading as it governs writing, and reading is therefore a miswriting just as writing is a misreading. As literary history lengthens, all poetry necessarily becomes verse-criticism, just as all criticism becomes prose poetry.

Having thus decreed poetry and criticism equals, he next proceeds to exemplify the absolute superiority of criticism over poetry in his own person, as he engages in hand-to-hand combat with the great dead poets of the past, using his Kabbalah to trip them, his sophism to subdue them and his various tropes to tie them up, head to foot. But before indulging ourselves in the awesome spectacle of Bloom engaging in this literary mud-wrestling, we should note to what extent he has already bested the balanced, constructive commentator in himself that we have seen earlier. Whereas before he had thought it wise to accept Freud's warning "that less than all had better content man" (Introduction to *The Ringers in the Tower,* written in 1969), now it is the "all" and only the "all" that will content Professor Bloom. In the years that were to follow, Bloom's ambitions became more feral and bestial, his appetites for power more omnivorous and his personal will more usurpatory and all-devouring.

By 1973 in *The Anxiety of Influence,* he began to absorb his own "strong precursors" to act out the demonics of his own Theory as the one and only way to ultimate strength and priority, like the emerging male gorilla who must physically subdue the herd leader to become a leader himself:

> Nietzsche and Freud are, so far as I can tell, the prime influences upon the theory of influence presented in this book. . . . Yet, the theory of influence expounded here is un–Nietzschean in its deliberate literalism, and in its Viconian insistence that priority in divination is crucial for every strong poet, lest he dwindle merely into a latecomer. My theory rejects also the qualified Freudian optimism that happy substitution is possible, that a second chance can save us from the repetitive quest for our earliest attachments.

Bloom here is in the process of absorbing his precursors, a process he completes in later books in time to achieve the "severity" and "priority" he needs to wrestle the great poets to the ground. Specifically, he is attacking Nietzsche for suggesting that Oedipal aggressions need not be acted out. Bloom's purposes, however, now demand that they be acted out to their fullest extent. Also, he has an old score to settle if he would turn Nietzsche aside so that we can behold Bloom himself untrammelled and unconfined as the sole exponent of the supremacy of criticism. Had not Nietzsche the audacity to write disparagingly of critics?

> The most astonishing works may be created; the swarm of historical neuters will always be in their place, ready to consider the author through their long telescopes. The echo is heard at once, but always in the form of "criticism," though the critic never dreamed of the work's possibility a moment before. It never comes to have an influence, but only a criticism; and the criticism itself has no influence, but only breeds another criticism. And so we come to consider the fact of many critics as a mark of failure. Actually everything remains in the old condition, even in the presence of such "influence": men talk a little while of a new thing, and then of some other new thing, and in the meantime they do what they have always done. The historical

training of our critics prevents their having an influence in the true sense — an influence on life and action.

Nietzsche's words are a taunting red flag to the new bull of battle in Bloom. As for Freud, Bloom singles out his notion of sublimation as the point of attack on the Viennese master: "Freud recognized sublimation as the highest human achievement, a recognition that allies him to Plato and to the entire moral traditions of both Judaism and Christianity. Freudian sublimation involves the yielding-up of more primordial for more refined modes of pleasure, which is to exalt the second chance above the first. Freud's poem, in the view of this book, is not severe enough...." In other words, Bloom would have us forego sublimation and act out the primordial urges of the unconscious. This of course is impossible this side of madness. Were it possible, there would be only one side to Bloom's primal words. Where there had been love-hate, peace-war, life-death, there would now be hate, war, death. This is the part of us his Theory would exercise. What were in *The Anxiety of Influence* tentative challenges become by the time of *Poetry and Repression* struggles to the death.

Bloom's magic weapon in all this will be the *syncretism* that he borrowed from Gnosticism and Kabbalah, which as I have said is to logical description as cancer is to a healthy body. Bloom prepares us for this in *A Map of Misreading* (page 128):

> Milton's full relation to Spenser is too complex and hidden for any rapid description or analysis to suffice, even for my limited purposes in this book. Here I will venture that Milton's transumptive stance in regard to all his precursors, including Spenser, is founded on Spenser's resourceful and bewildering (even Joycean) way of subsuming his precursors, particularly Virgil, through his labyrinthian syncretism.

So be prepared to be bewildered as we proceed to Bloom's absorption of Keats, as he abstracts the young bard and his great work from the context of Keats's life and intentions to make both seem the product of his, Bloom's, Theory. Through this device Bloom can come to control the entire known literary world, no matter how he has to shrink it, by absorbing the past, containing the present and anticipating the incursions of the future, long enough anyway to insure his tenure in academia and the great power and money that will accrue as a result.

By the time the future penetrates the armament of his thick-mailed,

Teutonic argument to the soft, white, freckled personal motives that puff beneath the metal garment, Bloom will have moved to new ground. Anticipating the mounting tempo of the attacks upon his Theory, in order to maintain his "priority," or dominance, he will become his own severest critic, throwing out the entire Theory of Anxiety of Influence and restoring his work to the mainstream of criticism where it will be immune to exception and disparagement. This should keep us all busy for another twenty years, when we can return to square one where we began before Bloom took over English literature at Yale.

Bloom's syncretism is invoked for many reasons. He senses that the wild "revisions" of *Poetry and Repression* (1976) may strike some people as somewhat insane. Through what he would call a prolepsis (anticipatory trope), he would allay any suspicions as to the soundness of the commentator's mind by stating prior to the reader's reaction any doubts he might encounter. This is, again, a sophist device, one that Bloom uses frequently in *The Anxiety of Influence:*

> Some of the consequences of what I am saying dismay even me. Thus, it cheers *me* up to say that the misreading of Milton's Satan by Blake and Shelley is a lot stronger than the misreading of Satan by C. S. Lewis or Charles Williams, let alone than the pitifully weak misreading of Satan by T. S. Eliot. But I am rather downcast when I reflect that the misreading of Blake and Shelley by Yeats is a lot stronger than the misreading of Blake and Shelley by Bloom.

So you see if you begin to suspect that Bloom's onslaught against prior poets and other critics might betoken a megalomania bordering on psychosis, he reduces himself to the normal proportions of a fallible human being from time to time, to win the reader's support for what turn out to be even more outlandish attacks just ahead. The more extreme he becomes, the more apt he is to adopt this friendly, intimate, highly sociable tone to offset any alarm on the part of the reader. This usually takes the form it does in regard to Milton's Satan, where he confesses his misreading may be too strong, or not strong enough, but it never leads him to the conclusion that a balanced reader may have reached long ago: the Theory itself is an example of psychoneurotic excess greater than any it might produce in others who employ it. And you can also see what Bloom envisions here, a prospect that I understand has already become an abiding reality at Yale: scores of young apprentices, or ephebes, mastering Bloom's Theory and in the process submitting their misreadings of great poets, or lesser ones for a change of pace, to have them judged and compared in terms of their various strengths and weaknesses.

Having absorbed his precursors in criticism by advancing his "strong" revisions against their weak standard critiques to become the most influential literary commentator in the English-speaking world, possibly in the history of criticism, Bloom now moves toward the final phase of his master plan, to overwhelm in the name of criticism the primacy of poetry itself. In *Poetry and Repression* (1976), he at last implements his own fantastic belief, that immortality, or a place in the sun, can only be secured by the Oedipal conquest of one writer (poet and critic have become interchangeable to him, you will remember) over his strongest precursor: "Poetic strength comes only from a triumphant wrestling with the greatest of the dead..." (*A Map of Misreading*, page 9).

In *Poetry and Repression,* like one possessed, he rushes headlong to the high ground of the sublime where the reputations of "the greatest of the dead" preside, and levels his theory at full tilt against them, plunging about the pantheon in an apparent frenzy to bend their meanings to fit within the coils of the Kabbalah and to reduce the poets themselves to automatons in the grip of *The Anxiety of Influence.* His purpose is to make it appear that their poems were written out of his Theory. Thus with one blow he would remove from himself the stigma of belatedness and from criticism the onus of being secondary, or in other words, to bring to himself and criticism priority over both poets and poetry. If Bloom's arguments seemed to rigidify in the books that immediately followed *The Anxiety of Influence,* in *Poetry and Repression,* the keystone of all he would erect, his theoretical structure has become so defiant of logic and gravity that he must improvise frantically to prevent its collapse on every side.

Milton and Wordsworth both acknowledged debts to their precursors, Milton to Spenser and Wordsworth to Milton, though not with any anxiety in the Bloomian sense. Milton felt a great intellectual and spiritual responsibility to advance Spenser's meanings through the modifications of his own century. And Wordsworth looked to Milton as a poetic and spiritual father, who did not cast him into Oedipal terror but rather sustained him, perhaps ambiguously, but in a traditional and healthy way in the manner of a father. Bloom then does not have much trouble reinforcing his Theory through their examples. But right up ahead is Bloom's nemesis, Keats, who must be disfigured beyond recognition if Bloom is to achieve his own sovereignty.

Bloom has an uncanny knack for appearing all-inclusive and at the same time avoiding contests that are not weighted in his favor, as in the case of Shakespeare. There is no doubt that he would if he could let Keats pass, too, beyond the reach of his Theory. But he cannot. The Theory must satisfy all the stereotypical "preconceptions" of criticism, and one of the most inevitable and unavoidable of these is that Keats is the mediating presence between the idealism of the Early Renaissance and the existentiality of our own Later Renaissance. Bloom must deal with him. And Bloom's problems are great.

Keats was and remains, like Shakespeare, a stubborn example of a poet who rebukes Bloom's Theory, as a product not of his predecessors or precursors but of the priority of the preemptive sensuous reality immediately around him. Keats dealt with the priority of other poets, but his own presence was such that he experienced comfort and not anxiety from their priority. Other poets did not bar his own entry into the sublime, as Bloom's Theory would *absolutely* insist. Rather they made his way easier; they welcomed him to their company, as we see in *On First Looking into Chapman's Homer,* Keats's first major rumination on the matter. Keats is more typical of the many, many great poets who remain intractable within Bloom's Theory, not as exceptions like Shakespeare, because they absorbed precursors, but as exceptions like Keats, because they regarded their own priority and immortality as being inclusive of all humanity and by that token not exclusive of any poet whether prior or belated.

Before *The Anxiety of Influence,* Bloom tended to regard Keats as a case aside as he did Shakespeare:

> That Keats had the healthiest of imaginations, balanced at last in a harmony of its own impulses, is now generally and rightly believed. The world of Keats is our world as Shakespeare's is, at once actual and visionary, sensuous, probable, yet open to possibility. From the *Ode to Psyche* on, it is accurate to say of Keats that his consciousness and imagination were one, and his sense of actuality absolute. He was refreshingly free of existing conceptions of the world, and free also of apocalyptic desire, the inner necessity that compelled Blake and Shelley to create their radical but open conceptions of possible worlds. The presence of death heightened Keats's imaginative naturalism by giving it relentless urgency, without persuading Keats that the earth was less than enough.
>
> Keats's sensible and yet highly sensitized Stoicism is one of Poetry's greatest monuments to its own effects as a viable and inspiring strategy for life itself. Keats refused to limit his person or his poetry with didactic absolutes, so that he might represent the Universality of

Poetry, its denial of historical disunities. His uncluttered presence in posterity stands as a crucial mediating figure for the future of the free and universal spirit to which the world has aspired for three millennia.

Bloom saw this twenty years ago. That the archcritic should abandon his total vision of Keats and attempt to reduce him to just another corrupted body in his syncretic, cancerous Theory's progression offers the most damning testimony of Bloom's own infection by the desperate lust for personal power. Even as late as *The Anxiety of Influence,* Bloom can note the great power of Keats's *The Fall of Hyperion,* and enthuse: "What is sublimated here is the most integral instance of a sensuous imagination since Shakespeare's." Only three years were to pass, however, before Bloom was ready in *Poetry and Repression* to subvert his own earlier elevation of Keats as one who attempted a universality free of "existing conceptions of the world." Bloom is then ready to burden Keats with all sorts of preconceptions, conscious and unconscious, to make him seem a mere functionary doing errands for his desperate Theory. Vowing to give the stoic Keats wider meaning than heretofore, the sophist Bloom in fact strips him of the garment of pure individuality that Keats had prepared for his own posterity. Bloom reduces him finally, as he had the others, to the mean necessities of the mortal condition, as one demonized by his envy of his precursors, entrapped by the anxiety of his own drive for personal supremacy in the poetic realm. By thus absorbing Keats, of course, Bloom achieves his own domination of the sublime, his own lifetime ambition, thus attaining at least purportedly the "priority," the supremacy of criticism over poetry for the first time in the history of English literature.

To do this, however, Bloom must bend logic beyond recognition. He returns for what must be his ultimate *reductio* in "Keats: Romance Revised" in *Poetry and Repression* (1976). In minimizing Keats, Bloom must first undermine the lofty critiques of his fellow critics. Among these is Paul de Man, one of Bloom's coworkers at Yale. I am not at all surprised that Bloom would disparage the work of a colleague, no matter how close he had been to him. Bloom's ambitions are transparent and his behavior predictable. I hope I am not being merely self-laudatory in pointing out here that I could predict the kind of attack that Bloom makes on Paul de Man, even as he reaches to sully the brilliance of Keats's posterity. At a time when I had read nothing that Bloom had written and had for guidance only one article by Hilton Kramer in the *New York Times Book Review,* I was able to project this in *A Modern Dunciad* (1977; in the poem, the Goddess Dullness has just announced her contest for the critics at the Old Belvedere Castle in Central Park. Bloom is on the parapet in the spotlight, as we behold his constitutional inclination):

> Still, Bloom in tux, a beacon from the wall,
> Spread wide his arms, to greet, and upstage all!

The Goddess holds forth a little longer and then:

> With this, she "threw it all" to mighty Bloom!
> Who waved de Man aside to make some room
> And placed his students with their Yalie stripes
> By height to either side like organ pipes,
> And then for pear-shaped tones and breath control,
> Did several knee-bends and "a mattress roll,"
> Turned-up the mike, and opened wide "the Bible,"
> That tome of his entitled *Bloom's Large Libel!*
> With this obnoxious, single crack-pot book,
> Hal ripped the ivy from its "crannied nook"!
> By claiming that "misreadings" of the text
> Would help us tell one critic from the next!
> Contempt for sense, he said, would make them stoic;
> The worse the error, O, the more heroic!"

As I say, at the time I had read only a brief article on Bloom by Hilton Kramer, that I will refer to later, in which there was no reference to any attack actual or prospective by Bloom upon de Man or any other of his colleagues. I mention this and quote the portion of *A Modern Dunciad* to show that such predictions as to behavior are possible when the subject is the incarnation of personal ambition as Bloom assuredly was and remains. We will have occasion again to predict his future actions as his career moves into its final stages. From the above, we derive hope that the predictions may have some validity and bear some resemblance to what he actually must do to sustain his own self-importance in the academic world. But back to our story and the combat to the death between criticism in the person of Bloom and poetry in the posterity of Keats.

To make his subjugation of Keats more colorful and palatable, Bloom will also wrestle with Paul de Man as the representative of traditional criticism. This way he can vivify his struggle by staging it with a then-living critic presumably his equal and at the same time minimize the onus that might attach to a combat with the pathetic ghost of Keats alone. By taking on de Man and his conventional critique of Keats, Bloom can widen the meaning of his victory to include all conventional criticism along with de Man and Keats within the circle of his conquest. This of course serves to reinforce Bloom's own conviction, which must at this point have become tenuous, that all this wrestling with the dead really means something in the last analysis. By bringing de Man into the picture, Bloom, sophist-like, is extending his psychodrama to the galleries at Yale, where de Man also taught, and at the same time implies that the outcome of his struggle is crucial to the ongoing critical wars of our time, and the future of criticism in general, in the entire English-speaking world. We should also note how Bloom, like the lumpy python, will advance the ingestion of both philosophy in the person of Nietzsche and psychology in Freud and Wollheim even further as he moves toward the total absorption of Keats into his Theory.

The arena for all this, as I say, is Chapter 5, "Keats: Romance Revised," in *Poetry and Repression*. So Bloom begins:

> Paul de Man engagingly remarks that "it is one of Keats's most engag-ing traits that he resists all temptation to see himself as the hero of a tragic adventure." De Man says also of Keats that "he lived almost always oriented toward the future," the pattern of his work being thus "prospective rather than retrospective." These are moving observa-tions, and I honor them. They surmise a Keats whose vision "consists of hopeful preparations, anticipations of future power rather than meditative reflections on past moments of insight and harmony." As does Angus Fletcher, de Man sees Keats as one of the *liminal* vi-sionaries, akin surely to Coleridge, to Hart Crane, perhaps to an aspect of Stevens. De Man points to all those phrases in Keats's poems and letters that "suggest he has reached a threshold, penetrated to the borderline of a new region which he is not yet ready to explore but toward which all his future efforts will be directed." If de Man were wholly right, then Keats ought to be happily free of the Shadow of Milton and of Wordsworth, the composite precursor that both in-spired and inhibited him. There can be no more extreme posture of the spirit, for a strong poet, than to take up perpetually, a prospective stance. I regret taking up a more suspicious or demystifying stance than de Man does, but Keats can charm even the subtlest and most scrupulous of deconstructors. No strong poet, of necessity, is wholly liminal in his vision, and Keats was a very strong poet, greatly gifted in the revisionary arts of misprision. I begin therefore by suggesting that de Man's observation accurately describes one of Keats's prime composite tropes, but also declines (on de Manian principle, of course) to examine the psychic defenses that inform Keats's liminal trope.

Thus Bloom brings Keats's spirit down to earth for what he calls "demystification," but which is in fact a trivialization beneath the compactor-like mechanisms of his Theory.

Anticipating the reader's capacity for disgust, as before, Bloom now adopts his conciliatory tone: "In reading Keats as having been a revisionist of Romance, I need to commence by the way I have read him in the past, for he too has suffered, and from other critics as well as myself, by the kinds of canon-misreading that canon-formation enforces." So you see, contrary to what you may sense, Bloom is not perpetrating a wrong in his revised revision of the Bard but correcting one. Thus the sophist lays his coils. We are now ready for a few breezy side trips, where we might test the *Map of Misreading* before we get to the important business at hand, the atomization of the integral figure of Keats in English literature:

> Let me return to, and now adumbrate, a distinction I ventured in *A Map of Misreading,* between ratios (tropes, defenses, images) of limitation and ratios of representation. I said there that "limitations turn away from a lost or mourned object towards either the substitute or the mourning subject, while representations turn back towards restoring the powers that desired and possessed the object."

If I am trying your patience here, it is nothing compared with what Bloom will do once he beguiles you into the wilderness of his *Map of Misreading.* Also, if you are not sure of just what he is saying most of the time, this is fine preparation for his conclusions, which make even less sense. Like the great Kabbalist he is, he finds certain refuge in the doubletalk of the two-way, reversible proposition, which he calls a ratio to suggest the precision of mathematics just long enough to intimidate the reader into suspending his own common sense and disbelief at what is taking place, not to mention his incredulity at all this nonsense. In doing literary history the great service of "demystifying" Keats, Bloom adorns himself and his own Theory with more mystification than might have attended the dawn of creation.

Thus robed in a sublime and sparkling light, he is ready to plunge further into the arcane equations of the Kabbalistic *A Map of Misreading:* "Representation points to a lack, just as limitation does, but in a way that *re-finds* what could fill the lack." What all this has to do with poor Keats we will never know. What does Bloom mean by the sentence just quoted? He means this: "Or, more simply: tropes of limitation also represent, of course, but they tend to limit the demands placed upon language by pointing to a lack both in language and the self, so that limitation really means recognition in this context. Tropes of representation also acknowledge a limit, point to a lack, but they tend to strengthen both language and the self." That's what he means.

Get it? If you stare at it long enough and read it against the categories in the *Map of Misreading,* meaning itself will lose its meaning. Another plus for Bloom's Theory! Now we are almost sufficiently disoriented to get to Keats himself. But Bloom would now test us by the final rigors of his revisionary ratios. Parental Guidance is advised here:

> The fundamental principle of an antithetical or Kabbalistic criticism is that, in poetic texts, tropes are best understood as psychic defenses, because they act as defenses, against the tropes of anteriority, against the poems of the precursors. Similarly, in poetic texts, the poet's (or his surrogate's) psychic defenses are best understood as tropes, for they trope or turn against anterior defenses, against previous or outworn postures of the spirit.

Whoever killed John Keats did it none too soon if it spared him this.

Bloom has always been inclined to compare the creation of literature to both the act of war and the act of sexual love. Ready for war with Keats, the critic now waxes warm and amorous as he moves toward the battle: "The problem of the status and significance of poetry must be resolved at last in the area where the understanding of the following will meet: dreaming, and the telling of dreams in poetry, and the analogy: sex, and the telling of sex in love. The dialectic of Romantic love, which involves dream and identity, is the core problem." The "dialectic" of Romantic love, "the core problem"? My God, what a date he turns out to be! Anyway, there's more — much more: "Is there an analogy between the strong poet's desire for priority and the motives or necessity for *telling,* whether of dreams in poetry or sexuality in love? We border on the realm of solipsism again; priority perhaps means not being first, but being alone, and is the demonic form of the apocalyptic impulse to be integrated again."

By this time Bloom has moved Keats through major portions of the bard's *The Fall of Hyperion.* He now breaks him up into little pieces and desperately attempts to find a precursor for the kind of experiences that Keats is undergoing. "In lines 81–181 of 'The Fall of Hyperion' Keats confronts his muse in a state of heightened awareness, but also in a state of reified vulnerability. The Keatsian *kenosis* [the third of six revisionary ratios] is neither a Wordsworthian regression nor a Shelleyan undoing, but rather resembles Stevens, Keats's descendant, in being a radical isolation."

Finding both Wordsworth and Shelley unproductive of the influence on Keats that Bloom needs to absorb him into his Theory,

Bloom temporarily settles for Stevens as Keats's prime precursor. The fact that Stevens comes after Keats in historical chronology should give us no trouble at this point, since Bloom has gone to great lengths to show us that, just as poems don't exist except as other poems, time does not exist either except as some other time in the strange cosmos of his Theory. Having failed to find a precursor influence strong enough to force Keats to behave in the manner mandated by his Theory, Bloom pushes the syncretism of the Kabbalah into a totally ungrounded realm to maintain the integrity of his Theory. Since Keats seems somehow immune to the influence of others, Bloom now forces the poet to confront *his own self* as the anxiety-producing precursor. Bloom forces Keats to misinterpret himself through one of the characters he has created in *The Fall of Hyperion* and in this way attain the sublime of immortality he could not otherwise.

So, in Keats, Bloom's strange Theory produces the bizarre spectacle of a poet chafing under the anxiety derived from his own influence upon himself. Thus, lacking any other mechanism, Bloom's Theory of Poetry, which was supposed to do away with both the tautologies and reductions of standard criticism, now gives us the anxiety of influence upon a poet troping and defending himself against his own shadow. Now is this a tautology, Bloom, old boy, or a reduction, or a little bit of both to make it a new kind of trope altogether? I think this calls for another quick book, revising all previous revisions.

In any case, for the first time, we learn that the poet needs no precursor to experience anxiety and to be under the influence. And now the poet does not need a precursor to misread or misinterpret. Now he can simply misread or misinterpret himself, if he happens to get in his own way en route to priority within the realm of the sublime. And the meaning of a poem, which had been defined as the variance between a belated text and a prior one by a precursor, can now be found in the variance between what a poet says here and what he says over there.

We have a new chaos within the sphere of the Kabbalah. Thus *The Anxiety of Influence: A Theory of Poetry* is cut off from its empirical foundations. But this cannot matter to the Kabbalist who insists on entering history here. And it cannot matter to the sophist who will overwhelm you at any and all costs, even if he has to turn John Keats into Fanny Farmer. And it does not matter to Bloom. He must have Keats under the bib of his Theory and Keats he will have:

I suggest that Keats, a startlingly clear intellect, has a proleptic understanding that there is no breakthrough to poetic strength without a double distortion, a distortion of the precursors, and so, of tradition, and a self-distortion in compensation. There is no growth into poetic strength without a radical act of interpretation that is always a distortion or misprision and, more subtly, without the necessity of so stationing the poet's ontological self that it too is held up to an interpretation that necessarily will also be distortion or misprision. Keats differs only in degree from previous strong poets by his *acceptance* of these necessities. The prime function of Moneta in the poem is to *misinterpret* Keats, but by so misinterpreting she canonizes him, in a dialectical reversal of her attitude that I now would say does not leave her at the end misunderstanding him any less radically than she misunderstands him when first he stands before her purgatorial stairs.

Having thus set Keats to wrestling with himself as his own intimidating predecessor, Bloom is now ready for the final truncation of Keats's monumental posterity. But prior to that ultimate act, Bloom must, as it were, totalize himself as the critic who would widen the domain of poetry, about to become his own, to include that of both philosophy and psychology. He will as he proceeds revise and complete Wollheim and Freud:

> A poem, as Freud well knew, was not a dream, nor a joke, nor a symptom. But Freud, as a humanistic scientist, and Wollheim, as an analytical philosopher, do not know that a poem *is* a kind of error, a beautiful mistake or open lie, that does have the function of, somehow, telling a dream. Wollheim, following and expounding Freud, says that a poem does not avail itself of a drop in consciousness or attention in order to become the vehicle of buried desires. But here I think Wollheim is not close enough to what poems actually do, perhaps because he is more interested in the visual arts and less in poetry. Poems, I would insist, indeed do just the reverse of what Wollheim says they don't do, but as this is a dialectical reversal it too is frequently reversed, and so poems do refute Wollheim, not in theory but in the ways they behave. It is by the mode of sublimity that poems suddenly do become the vehicle of buried desires, by violent heightenings of consciousness or attention. But these heightenings can drop away just as suddenly, and abandon us to the consequences of repression, a process rhetorically manifested through the substitution of the trope of litotes for that of hyperbole, by turning to an underthrow of language that plunges us from the Sublime down into its dialectical brother, the Grotesque.

Did you once think that criticism should heighten your awareness of the poem? Obviously, if Bloom has his way, you have forgotten both the poem and the poet altogether, to concentrate without distraction upon the dialectical pyrotechnics of the Great Kabbalistic Critic, who now moves to bend Freud and Keats to the purposes of the Kabbalah with one stroke:

> Wollheim usefully adds that there is a gap in Freud's account of art, a gap that I think a more antithetical criticism of poetry can help to fill. . . . Wollheim remarks: "In a number of celebrated passages Freud equated art with recovery or reparation on the path back to reality. But nowhere did he indicate the mechanism by which this came about. By the time he found himself theoretically in a position to do so, the necessary resources of leisure and energy were, we must believe, no longer available to him."

No problem, Bloom will do it for him!

> It is in the absence of this third-stage Freudian model that I have proposed a Kabbalistic model or paradigm [Bloom bubbles, rushing helpfully to Freud's elbow], for the image-patterning, for the movement of tropes and defenses towards the strengthening of the poetic ego, that I think is characteristic of the major poets of the last several centuries. . . . [W]e can distinguish between a poem and a dream or unconscious process, simply by remarking that the dream or unconscious process is overdetermined in its *meanings,* since we are discovering, if I am right, that belated poems suffer an increasing overdetermination in *language,* but an increasing *under-determination in meaning.* The dream or the symptom has a redundancy of meaning, but the Wordsworthian or modern poem has an apparent dearth of meaning, which paradoxically is its peculiar strength, and its demand upon and its challenge to, the interpretative powers of the reader.

Here Bloom again invites his Master Reader, or his *Überleser* to share in the great gala of misreading Keats: "This fictive reader simultaneously somehow negatively fulfills and yet exuberantly transcends self, much as Zarathustra so contradictorily performed. Such a reader, at once blind and transparent with light, self-deconstructed yet fully knowing the pain of his separation from both text and from nature, doubtless will be more than equal to the revisionary labors of contradiction and destruction . . ." (*A Map of Misreading,* page 5). The reader's work is cut out for him:

> There is no subject *of* the poem or *in* the poem, nor can we make the poem into its own subject. There is a dearth of meaning in a strong poem, a dearth so great that, as Emerson says, the strong poem forces us to invent if we are to read well, or as I would say, if we are to make our misreading stronger and more necessary than other misreadings.

"The Fall of Hyperion" is a very strong poem because it impels every reader to return upon his or her enterprise as a reader. That is the challenge Keats gives us: his stance in relation to Moneta, which means to tradition, which means in turn to the composite precursor, becomes the inevitable paradigm for our stance as readers in relation to the text.

Bloom would have us, *Überlesers* all, share his own desperation in the matter of misreading, neglecting the fact that he himself is unique in his Kabbalistic ambition to dominate the text and that most of us can survive better by identifying with Keats without trying to absorb him and assume priority over him through our misreading, revision or misinterpretation of what has been so passionately and ingeniously constructed. Keats's universality lies in the inspiring nature of his own stoicism in the face of cosmological uncertainty. We as readers can quickly identify with such common and yet worthy human behavior. It is not our task as readers to "trope" or "defend" ourselves against Keats's priority, but to enter into it and share it as it has been given life by his own great poetic imagination.

To fracture the integrity of Keats's experience through Bloomian dialectics is to smash the well-wrought urn. That Keats himself would not have it so and is a guide highly preferable to Bloom himself in matters of this kind, there can be no doubt whatsoever: "At once it struck me," Keats writes, "what quality went to form a man of achievement, especially in literature, and which Shakespeare possessed so enormously — I mean *negative capability,* that is when a man is capable of being in uncertainties, mysteries, doubts, without any irritable reaching after fact or reason." Bloom would obliterate outright the humanizing, chastening condition of cosmic uncertainty and reduce the great mystery of human creation to a paltry phantasmagoric rationalization. And Keats writes again: "Poetry should surprise by a fine excess, and not by singularity. It should strike the reader as a wording of his own highest thoughts, and appear as almost a remembrance." (Both quotes are from Keats's letters.)

In other words, poetry should invoke the fixed Kantian categories or Jungian archetypes of the mind. Why then, or how can we escape its categorical meaning by imposing upon it an arbitrary or merely interpretive meaning through our efforts to stand aside from it, to modify it and finally to do away with it altogether, when in fact it is part of us and part of nature? Yet this is what Bloom is calling on us to do:

> This late in tradition, we all come to one another smothered in and
> by meaning; we die daily, facing one another, of our endlessly mutual
> interpretations, self-interpretations. We deceive ourselves, or are
> deceived, into thinking that if only we could be interpreted rightly, or
> interpret others rightly, then all yet would be well. But by now — after
> Nietzsche, Marx, Freud and all their followers and revisionists —
> surely we secretly — all of us — know better. We know that we must be
> misinterpreted in order to bear living, just as we know we must mis-
> interpret others if they are to stay alive, in more than the merely
> minimal sense. The necessity of misreading one another is the other
> daily necessity that accompanies sleep and food, or that is as pervasive
> as light and air. There is no paradox in what I am saying. . . .

No paradox? Who on earth would agree? There is much paradox in
what he is saying. And more of madness itself. Any theory that would
win the support of history must have about it the aura of necessity and
inevitability. Bloom's has nothing of this. I doubt that anyone else,
given a hundred million years, would come to the conclusion that the
only way he could survive was to be misunderstood and the only way
he could sustain others was to misunderstand them. This is a
gratuitous eccentricity, to say the least. Anyone who tries to practice
it according to Bloom's advisories would be thrown swiftly in jail. That
should be the greatest proof of its perversity.

So much for it! Having made his bid for the Golden Bomb Award
of the Century, Bloom now moves to his final deflation of Keats:

> I would transpose Freud's formula of negation into the realm of
> poetry, and specifically into the context of "The Fall of Hyperion," by
> suggesting that, in Keats's poem, Moneta, as what Freud calls the
> symbol of negation, mediates for Keats not so as to free his thought
> from the consequences of repression but so as to show him that his
> thought cannot be so liberated, if it is to remain *poetic* thought. When
> she has shown Keats this, then it is his heroism that permits him to
> accept such dark wisdom. Romance, as Keats teaches us to under-
> stand it, cannot break out of the domain of the pleasure-principle even
> though that means, as Keats knows, that romance must accept the vi-
> sion of an endless entropy as its fate.

So Bloom, having gratuitously determined that Keats was not a god,
as in fact the poet had no inclination to be, somehow deprives him
even of his sensible humanity, making him seem instead a doomed
soul entrapped in his own fatuousness. Bloom has removed the fine
young bard from the crest of the sublime, where Bloom has told us
there is room for only one, Bloom himself: "In Keats, the repetition
of romance becomes the perpetual and difficult possibility of *becoming*

a strong poet. When Keats persuaded himself that he had mastered such repetition, *as a principle,* then "The Fall of Hyperion" broke off, being as finished a poem as a strong poem can be. Keats had reached the outer threshold of romance, and declined to cross over it into the realm of tragedy."

Had Keats lived long enough to write the dramas he aspired to and thus "cross over into the realm of tragedy," Bloom could not have followed him there for a new, revised fitting of his Theory. Drama, poetic or otherwise, unlike the lyric, is preempted by the interplay of character within social structures. The influence of precursors pales to nothingness against the withering priority of actuality. A desire to be first in love, war and poetry is like a case of puppy love. In a healthy mind, such onanism cannot sustain a man through the trials of his later years. To dwell upon it as Bloom does is to forsake all the conditions of real spiritual development. Obviously, his own ambitions have led him to his Macbeth-like depredations and the obsessiveness that issues from all these figurative critical murders.

But just as Bloom realized that his Theory cannot deal with poetry as either a craft or a system of ethics as represented by Shakespeare's poetry, he also knows it cannot be applied to behavior in the real world we all finally inhabit. In other words, it cannot serve as a real ethic or principle of behavior, but only as a posture or a position or a stance within the cardboard world of academia. There, however, it serves Bloom's purposes beautifully. You will remember that he began his chapter on Keats by citing de Man's insistence "that it is one of Keats's most engaging traits that he resists all temptation to see himself as the hero of a tragic adventure" and that Keats "lived almost always oriented toward the future."

Having thus demonstrated his own personal priority over Keats and the priority of Criticism over Poetry, Bloom in passing also gives de Man his lashes: "Poised there, on the threshold, his [Keats's] stance is more retrospective than he could have wanted it to be, but there he remains still, in a stance uniquely heroic, in despite of himself." And, we might add, in despite of de Man's assertions to the contrary and in despite of the lesser critic's expectations of a promotion. We should never forget, in this dialogue of sophists in academia, we the *Überlesers* are to be flattered but never taken seriously. These critics are really talking to themselves only. If the Yale Corporation, which dispenses raises and tenure, should overhear, well then, all has not been in vain!

Chapter II. Ashbery and Neo-Existential Poetry Step into a Void.

Harry Smith, publisher of *The Generalist Papers,* and I have been discussing the condition of modern poetry occasionally over bacon and eggs throughout the last fifteen years. As the dust settles finally into a fixed Egyptian desert, the villainous instruments protrude in the form of critic Harold Bloom and his poetic squire, John Ashbery, with a breathless assist to the stirrup by A. R. Ammons. Incidentally, this is the kind of mixed metaphor enclosed in a logical ellipse that John Ashbery thinks becomes the literary equivalent to Einstein's Theory of Relativity. This example, where the figures, first sensed as weapons or utensils in the sand, suddenly turn into a group of Crusaders, could be converted to an Ashberian stanza by simply deleting syntactical connectives and adding composite historic stereotypes softened, updated and diffused by blurring qualifiers and modifiers. It is left to the audience to emit the "oohs" and "ahs" to complete the tableau, which we shall call for handy reference: "Ashbery Vis-à-Vis His Reading Public." As to the question of Ashbery's poetry, you must believe me when I say, I feel we have beaten this animal to death. I would rather await history's removal of the horse's corse (corpse) from the scene, ass and all. But so much churns in the brain at the merest drop of the name — Ashbery! As Ashbery himself, in a poem whose place in his oeuvre I cannot right now pinpoint, imagines Wyatt and Surrey prancing to their task, murmuring "All this gorgeous material!", so I slog on through the shit despite myself. . .

The question remains: What has poetry lost since the Elizabethans and, more plainly, since the poetry of John Donne and the seven-

30

teenth-century Metaphysicals? What did verse contain back then in the way of human engagement, integration and guts that is so obviously lacking in postmodernist poetry? Only the reconstruction of a richer past in this respect can demonstrate by its contrast the inhospitable vacuity that characterizes current poetry as epitomized by today's laureates, Ashbery and Ammons. *Yes, what has been lost?* Once we batten upon that question, we run-on the even greater dilemma: How is postmodern poetry attempting to address the loss and replenish it?

And by the way, don't you love these new semiotic mysteries encapsuled in words like "postmodern"? "Modern" inviting the question, compared to what? And "postmodern" remoter still, around a bend we can no longer even see. Couldn't we also compound this question into a little Ashberian poem, contending it is the literary equivalent of genetic engineering? We could call it "Semiotics: A Doodle on the Meaning of Meaning," or perhaps more fetchingly, "Will-o'-My-Wisp." Or has Ashbery already written it? No, as I look it up, his poem with the equally fey title is labeled "Hop o' My Thumb" (*Self-Portrait in a Convex Mirror,* 1975, page 32).

Anyone who has practiced the craft of poetry as I have for fifty years, when undertaking such a consideration — what has been lost and how that loss is to be restored, if at all — cannot escape reference to his own "career" and the work therein, unprepossessing as it might be. Such a person cannot entirely escape all self-reference, cannot prevent the commingling of literary history with his own writings upon it and his own experiences of it. So if I seem to stray from the field for a moment or two, kindly indulge me. Simply chalk it up to a call of nature or a memory so gouged and gutted by ravines due to shock and gulleys due to sheer work (assonance of Swinburne!) that it favors the dispersal of fact over its confluence as the quickest way to the mainstream today. Now, how's that, John, as a replication in both form and substance of how you think you got where you are right now?

A television talk show was convened in July 1989, to comment on the huge retrospective of the late Andy Warhol's art at the Museum of Modern Art. One of the participants, art critic Hilton Kramer, struggled alone to point out what he thought the true meaning of the show was: In order to describe Andy Warhol's Factory products as great art, Kramer asserted, there first had to be a devaluation, a complete reduction of all great art that had come before. This staunch commentator used an analogy from urban development, or, rather from gentrification. In order to call these flimsy, glitzy condos and co-ops sprouting up all around us great architecture, Kramer said, in effect, you first have to redefine great architecture in terms that would equate it with the condos. This would exclude, he reasoned, all the great architecture of the past — that of Greece and Rome and the other great ancient empires, including those in the Orient, the awesome cathedrals of the Renaissance right down to the illustrious structures of our own time such as the Empire State Building, the Woolworth Building, the Seagram's Building and so on.

This same kind of reduction, of course, has actually occurred in poetry. It became manifest somewhere around the mid–1960s coincident with the despair of John Berryman (one of the last poets to attempt an accommodation with tradition) and the return of John Ashbery. Ashbery's self-removal to Paris (1956) had been a canny strategy of self-exile preparatory to a triumphant return. A footnote in my own *A Modern Dunciad* (1978) describes the literary scene in New York back then:

> Of his [Ashbery's] return to New York (1966), Richard Kostelanetz writes: "An unknown poet a decade before, he returned a conquering hero, sort of. During his absence, he was still a presence in New York. The art dealer Jill Kornblee remembers, 'Everybody talked about him as though he were in the room.' His reading at the Living Theatre drew a packed house. Kenneth Koch, by then a professor of English at Columbia University, had introduced Ashbery's work to his students; one of them, Jonathan Cott, wrote his first extended critical consideration of Ashbery's poetry for an anthology of criticism which I edited, *The New American Arts* (1965), in which Cott identified Ashbery as 'today's most radically original American poet.'" What a small world!

Ashbery was to state years later from the eminence of his chic success that he and his cohorts from Harvard, Yale and Columbia had consciously combined ("sort of") to write the "first modern poetry," ushering in a new literary era. This is described *in context* nowhere else except in a footnote to *A Modern Dunciad:* "Speaking of the early 1950s, Ashbery has said: 'We were all young and ambitious then. American painting seemed the most exciting art around. American poetry was very traditional at that time, and there was no modern poetry in the sense that there was modern painting.'" He meant that his aesthetic was based upon, not a mere break with the past, but a total disregard for it. As a veteran commentator upon the nonobjective visual arts, Ashbery had taken his cue from the Abstract Expressionists and carried over the fracture of representational elements and meaning to language. Many others, like Frank O'Hara, had done this. But it was left to Ashbery to proselytize and, with the assistance of his strategically positioned friends, to use the innovation as both a cause and an effect of a calamitous historic severance, or the reduction of all great works of literature — as a prelude to the invasion of the ersatz.

Based as it was upon the presumed inutility of all known literature that had come before, the new poetic models of Ashbery worked to contract the role of poetry in our cultural existence, to make it the special, exclusive province of initiates into third generation abstract painting, where the warped parallel was first generated. Finally the new poetic cult gained a life of its own within East Coast academic enclaves. Ashbery's strategy insists upon the isolation of aesthetics from the main body of philosophy. Those who reflexively look to his presence do not seem to realize what such a disconnection entails. In fact, it has emptied poetry of all meaning beyond itself, not only in philosophic categories such as ethics and metaphysics, but in the central cultural categories of sociology and politics as well. In other words, it precludes the nurturing elements of our very existence. Put bluntly, it erases history. An experiment perilous if there ever was one!

Meaning in American poetry has scattered and disappeared, as mercury, held in the palm and squeezed, slithers through the fingers. Traditional poetry throughout recorded time has proceeded from the efferent to the referent, from the subject to the figure of speech. Postmodern, Neo-Existential, or Ashberian verse reverses this logical categorical relationship. It places the referent at the active center of the poem with only a faint trace, or none at all, of the efferent — the object in question — that called it into being. This remains out of sight, or peripheral to the poem. Hence, the so-called "magic" of Ashbery's verse. Hence, the imputed "mystery" of the new poetry, inviting all sorts of ontological speculation that has sent verse in search of the "sublime" for the last fifty years, beginning with Wallace Stevens and ending — God, let's hope so! — with the platitudinous embroideries of Ashbery and Ammons.

What do I mean by the "referent as the center of the poem"? And by "platitudinous embroideries"? Any page of Ashbery's Pulitzer Prize–winning *Self-Portrait in a Convex Mirror* (1975) will provide us with an example, or rather a specimen informing the entire *genre,* as this from "The One Thing That Can Save America":

> These are connected to my version of America
> But the juice is elsewhere *[He means literally the orange juice-cum-puns]*
> This morning as I walked out of your room
> After breakfast crosshatched with
> Backward and forward glances, backward into light,
> Forward into unfamiliar light,
> Was it our doing, and was it
> The material, the lumber of life, or the lives
> We were measuring, counting?
> A mood soon to be forgotten
> In crossed girders of light, cool downtown shadow
> In this morning that has seized us again?

Those last two lines contain a feeble echo of Hart Crane's powerful *To Brooklyn Bridge,* wherein Crane wrote:

> Down Wall, from girder into street neon leaks,
> A rip-tooth of the sky's acetylene;
> All afternoon the cloud-flown derricks turn...
> The cables breathe the North Atlantic still.

The next stanza of Ashbery's poem evokes vacuum-packed reverberations of Crane's last great poem, *The Broken Tower,* written before his tragic suicide sixty years ago. Ashbery has mentioned that among his mentors are Stevens and Auden. But he has seldom if ever mentioned Hart Crane. Why? Is it because Ashbery could not fit Crane's powerful passions into the rigged optics of his own poetry? Or is it because Stevens and Auden enjoy an academic cachet that Crane never acquired? When, despite Ashbery's precious aversion, Crane is a much greater poet than either Stevens or Auden, assuming his place in the American pantheon, or the literary Rushmore, along with Dickinson, Poe and Whitman!

More of all this later. Meanwhile, in the examples above, note how the metaphor or referent in Crane is secondary to the expansive narrative line of the poem. It complements the real scene being described. Then look to see how the Ashbery parallel in the excerpt places the metaphor (a cross-hatched doodle) at the center of the poem, eliminating its efferent. As to substance, also note how Ashbery substitutes the petty inward pet between the poet and his pal for the great outreaching drama of all the Herculean constructions "downtown," the great batteries of human achievement in the buildings in the Wall Street area and the Brooklyn Bridge itself.

So the metaphor replaces the object as the sensory stimulant. In other words, the mere association becomes the agent of experience. Ashbery's poems rest on the memory of memory, memory's experience of itself. That's what all the Ashbery clappers mean when they marvel, "The poem is about itself." They will admit this to be solipsistic and then add, "It's a solipsistic age." But do they realize that it breaks down into a more pathological manifestation that is onanistic? That it is, in fact, a brand of self-paralyzing narcissism; that beneath that, it is compulsively masturbatory, or possibly as a more socially acceptable substitute, a compulsive form of homophilia? The objection is not to the sexual form, but to the poetic form that coyly jumbles up the entire universe simply to disguise what should not be hidden in truth — that is, in fact, far out-of-date in the "closet." Hart Crane was homosexual. So were Whitman, Housman and many others. But they did not allow this fact to thwart their poetic impulses by distorting their sense of immediate reality.

The Ashberian poets have sent reality packing, or asked the bellhop to forward it to their new address. Just what is the process here? You must forgive me if I bring forward excerpts from pieces I have written over the last fifteen years revealing just how this works. I doubt I will ever be able to say it more succinctly. As a backdrop for these excerpts, it should be understood that the triumph of the Ashberian model was complete by 1975, the year Ashbery won the Pulitzer Prize. The amazing thing is, no one in either the popular or academic press questioned the model. No one, as far I knew then or know now, has ever even analyzed it to describe its components. And, more crucially, no one seemed to even notice that the new *genre* of abstract poetry has literally knocked the stomach and heart out of the American literary tradition. And, setting the stage for the deranged literary epoch we are now experiencing, the model was back then, and still is, raised as the ideal for tens of thousands of students across the United States. Anticipating such consequences, I wrote a long piece on the problem for Harry Smith's now defunct *Newsart* (winter 1976) to document how much had really been surrendered to "postmodernism." The piece was entitled "Ashbery & Company — There Goes the Bathwater — Who's Got the Baby?" Excerpts:

> ... Current efforts to modernize poetry have failed to make a sharp distinction between those dead literary elements that can be safely cut away and such things as logic, syntax and coherent recall. The result

is inevitable: Important realities cannot be allowed to impinge upon the new poetry. Poems must either shock or mystify....

... Howard Moss binds his poetry within the tight predictable tautologies of philosophical Existentialism. Moss can be depended upon to go right over the mountain, possibly even straight off a cliff without looking up from the tips of his toes. He is important in all this, however, because he has been such an effective conduit [as poetry editor of *The New Yorker*] for the tableau poetry of [Malcolm] Brinnan and the painterly poetry of John Ashbery....

... It is John Ashbery, however, who has pushed what is essentially a fraudulent analogy between poetry and painting to its ultimate dead end....

... We should be aware of the basically simple reductions Ashbery manages when he uses atonal music or Dadaist painting as touchstones. But can we paint a picture or compose music that will be realized as poetry is realized? Or more to the point, should we set out to compose a poem that sacrifices all the unique virtues of poetry and puts in their place the effects of painting or of music? ...

... Ashbery surely must know that his vaunted analogy between abstract painting and a poetry that is modern by virtue of a similar nonobjectivity is an egregious fallacy. Words as the stuff of poetry and paint and line as the stuff of painting are in direct aesthetic opposition to one another. Ashbery's poetry shatters at the point of this opposition between the two. It doesn't explode to aesthetic effect. It crumbles, falls apart without releasing energy. Put any word on paper. It insists on the thing it represents, shape it as you will. Put a dab of paint or draw a line. You can call them nothing or shape them into anything you want....

Eight years later (1984) Ashbery's poetry had driven the collective American literary memory farther and farther out to sea. During that period, I strove to keep the shore in sight, to recall the small ground of support that poetry had enjoyed up to 1966. From the "Foreword" to my poem "Kelly's Grandchild" (*The Ballad of the Dollar Hotel and Other Poems*, 1984, Mountain Laurel Publications, Harrisburg, Pa.):

A few years ago [circa 1980] I wandered into the Salmagundi Club on Fifth Avenue in Greenwich Village and heard Nobel Nominee Jorge Luis Borges speak to a distinguished gathering of PEN (Poets, Essayists and Novelists). In the course of his talk, the esteemed poet and novelist told the American scribes they should pay more attention to the forsaken and neglected poets like Rudyard Kipling and A. E. Housman. Borges meant that poets should bring the narrative line back into American poetry. That's the only way they could reintroduce philosophy to their verse. Needless to say, philosophy embraces aesthetics (beauty), ethics (morality) and metaphysics (spirituality).

Borges was speaking against the tragic absence of all these qualities in the poetry being written by our laureates today. The Impressionist poetry of William Carlos Williams, sensible enough perhaps as a reaction to the heavy metaphysical burden of the poetry of Eliot, Pound and, to a lesser degree, Yeats, has in recent decades degenerated to the grudging gibberish of Ashbery and the vacuous, verbless maundering of Ammons. The highly remote, almost indecipherable content of this verse has remained of interest only to those who study it so they may become initiates in the elite academia where it is taught.

By divesting poetry of all substance and accessible meaning they have alienated the once-vast audience for American poetry. This is a cultural tragedy of the first magnitude. Borges was telling us that it need not be everlasting. That poets can bring back the narrative, reintroduce philosophy, reinvoke in their verse such ancient and efficacious fixtures as common sense, empathy, recall, and affectivity; and in the process get rid of the academic poets and win back the allegiance of society to the honorable causes of Homer and Shakespeare.

Despite such admonitions, throughout the second half of the last decade American poetry has become thinner and thinner, more and more remote, according to the rarification of the Ashberian model as exhibited in virtually annual new volumes of his verse. Taking the wrinkles and crimps out of the reasoning and structure of such poetry turned into a formal scholastic exercise that becomes an end in and of itself. The disconnection from the conduct of our daily existence is thus complete. Our leading poets do not acknowledge such a deficit. They struggle mutely, nonetheless, to indemnify their maturity, not to mention their old age, by striving to go beyond their lyric spasms to the more sustained strategies of the long narrative. They could not — and cannot — achieve this within their antithetical, aphilosophical aesthetic.

I stuck to my last, writing over and over again in various review pieces that the eradication of formal qualities, especially of common sense, logic and recall and the disciplines of sociology and politics, inevitably banished history from their poetry and made the narrative and epic impossible. In the long preface to my *Old Soldiers,* a 2,000-line narrative poem about the Pacific phase of World War II, this was one of the points I worked to clarify again:

> So is it any wonder that our distinctly inferior laureates today reach desperately for unproductive devices to expand their chronic lyric impulses into an epic narrative measure of some kind, Ginsberg with Buddhist musical accoutrements, Ashbery with a convex mirror and Merrill with a ouija board? All of them fail to integrate the substance

of contemporary history into their verse because they cannot perceive that the premise for doing so resides, not in exotic touchstones, but in the natural processes of epic poetry itself, as explicated so quickly and incisively by Aristotle more than two thousand years ago when he wrote that historical poetry is "a more philosophical and a higher thing than history: for poetry tends to express the universal, history the particular."

Since poets today do not see how current history can be worked into their verse, they say, of all things, that history is not important. Besides, they insist, objects and events that must be represented in their true delineations do not belong in poetry anyway. They look to painting for their authority to jumble-up appearances. Yet they feel the need to write an epic of some kind, to find some verbal equivalent for the great events that all but engulf them even as they remain remote from what they create. The principles of modern painting misapplied to poetry, combined with the philosophical eradications of Existentialism, have destroyed the modern poet's natural impulse toward epic poetry. A corollary of this: affectivity, or feeling, logic and common sense, hence ethics and justice, recall, even syntax, memory itself, all have been erased; ergo, history has disappeared from poetry even as it prepares to annihilate us.

So the erasure of literary tradition to make room for the dominance of the new model became total. The reduction generalized throughout academia and spread to abutting enclaves embracing literary salons and little magazines. As a consequence, the poet as an active heroic figure in the wider society has disappeared. Also, without traditional, or formal poetry, the vast scholastic paraphernalia of traditional criticism became a blighted branch of learning. Enter Harold Bloom, from his fiefdom at Yale, to hack his way to the high heroic ground once held by the poet, with (literally) cries of "Criticism is a battle to the death!"

Bloom had been watching developments in the arena of published poetry since the mid-1960s. He quietly appraised the weakness in the ranks of his fellow traditional critics occasioned by the new poetry. As Ashbery advanced and the social impact of poetry receded, Bloom literally leapt into the breach, first to dominate criticism, then to substitute criticism for poetry as the central literary experience of our epoch, clearing the way for an empty criticism in the form of Deconstruction to work in concert with the vacuity of Ashberian poetry.

The progression of this process as urged and finally effected by Bloom is detailed in Chapter I. In his dozen or so books, Bloom throws around a lot of soft, appealing, prestigious names plucked from the history of aesthetics (literature). This is to obscure the brass knuckles in his pulpy freckled fist. Be sure, within it, he has clenched the mugging device of the old Greek sophists to pulverize his unwitting opponents, his colleagues at Yale, and then the rest of the academics in the country. Having thrown the enemy (everyone connected to *any* literary tradition) on the defensive, Bloom finally launches his Blitzkrieg, leaving no doubt as to his monumental personal ambitions. He drops his bombshell, *The Anxiety of Influence: A Theory of Poetry* (1973). It was the final, decisive breakthrough following the feints and timid thrusts of his patsy poet, Ashbery. Two years later (1975), Ashbery got his Pulitzer, and Bloom became the most powerful figure in the History of American Letters.

Under Bloom, criticism becomes a poem, superior to the poem it criticizes. Both Bloom and his consort-queen in these new dominions, Helen Vendler at Harvard, dwell upon the *apparent* lack of meaning in the poetry of Ammons and Ashbery. It was the opening Bloom needed for his conquest. It later became Vendler's stock-in-trade at Harvard. Having leveled the known world of criticism, Bloom followed the easy road to total victory. It was just a question of mopping up, of setting up Ammons and Ashbery — and a couple of others like them — as poetic dummies or puppets to provide the semblance of continuity between criticism and poetry in the new state, where in fact there was none. The vital connection betweeen poetry and criticism had been replaced by the interchangeability of both through the dominant dogma of Deconstructionism.

Bloom's dialectic has turned the world of literature upside-down. What had been only tilted has been tipped right over on its head. Harold Bloom at Yale and Helen Vendler at Harvard. How axial! It had been Harvard that baptized Ashbery. Yale that confirmed him (with its annual Younger Poets award arbitrated by Auden in 1955). Bloom and Vendler, Ammons and Ashbery. Vendler and Bloom. Ashbery and Ammons. Year after year. Thousands of poems. Millions of words. Bloom on Ammons. Vendler on Ashbery. Bloom on Ashbery. Vendler on Ammons. Ashbery on Vendler. Ammons on Bloom. Ashbery on Bloom. Ammons on Vendler. Bloom on Vendler. Vendler on Bloom. Forty days and forty nights times twenty-five years (1965–1990). The flood covered everything. Common poetic ground vanished. Tradition sank. Formalistic critics and poets. Swept to oblivion. Postmodernism alone. On the holy peak. With Bloom and Vendler. Ashbery and Ammons. Money poured down. Prestige and power shone. Only on them.

Bloom crisscrossed the country. Checks at every stop. Bloom on the hustings. A powerful speaker system. Boomed. His books. Leapt from the presses. Like catechisms at the Vatican. I bought six of them. Bloom's books. At New York's Gotham Book Mart. In 1980. The stock boy pulled them from the shelf. Behind the empty space there were six more. The same books. They were double-stocked. There had been nothing like it. Never. In the history of Western Civilization. Bloom. Bloom and Vendler. Vendler. A small fish on Bloom's back. Rode far out. Gathered her essays into postmodernist tomes. Her words now glittered with fashion. In the glossy *New Yorker*. In the midst of fashion ads. The sheen of the negligees. The glow of the diamonds. The gleam of the silverware spread upon velvet. And within the heavy canonical folds. Of *The New York Review of Books*. Vendler. Cachet. Her essays. Ersatz. Set forth as jewels. On whom? Ashbery and Ammons.

Now Vendler was a big label. Bloom dove deeper to get rid of her. She could by then manage on her own. Stayed on the surface. Better for easy strokes. And longer distances. The newcomer's blush disappeared. Supplanted by an expert. Professorial smile. She rolled her hoop. From the splintered corridors of Boston U. To the plush green grass at Harvard. Had her own Heidelberg now. And her own Chair. Fuck off, Bloom! Her own Chair? Hell, her own *chaise-longue*. Vendler. Harvard's new William R. Kenen Professor of English. *And* American Literature. *And* Language.

Ashbery and Ammons. Ashbery blew up his doodles. Big frames. Victorian parlor art. Updated as Pop. Op. The equivalent of particle physics, his world thinks. Ashbery. Book-after-book. That open boyish face. Glowing through the blue lenses of bookstore windows. The sweater. And corduroys. The mustache smiling. Kindly. The lips serious. Just the right touch of severity. For the cryptic pose. The inscrutable remark. Profundity. Ashbery and Ammons. Ammons. The new big burp in Southern Backwaters. No Sidney Lanier here. Ammons. Dispatched James Dickey to a smaller pond. Ammons. Ploughed under. The Southern Agrarians. No exotic crops at his place. Just plain old American corn. Stripped of husks. No adjectives and adverbs. Only the kernels. Modern. The verbs would go next. The kernels themselves. What's left? Just the cob. Modern-Modern. Postmodern. Ask him. He'll tell you. A list of objects. God will he tell you! Collections of his collections. Everywhere.

Bloom made Ammons the standard decal at his Yale Deconstructionist Theme Park. Much money. Many monks. Shriven of the past. Shorn of the present. The new seminarians. Adepts at Deconstruction. Dispersed to spread the Word throughout academia. On a national scale. Ashbery and Ammons as subtexts in the new hagiography. Buried beneath Bloom's critical theories. They liked it down there. After all, poetry doesn't *do* anything. Just makes a few people rich. "Poetry doesn't make anything happen." Auden said so.

Robinson Jeffers said. Ya gotta know where poetry's going. And get there first. Bloom turned that cynical musing into a public battle cry. Ashbery? Well. Different. Shy. Like the Georgian poets. Upstaging the noisome Pre-Raphaelites. With a coy murmur.

Ashbery. Makes you turn up to him. Stagewise. His hands tentative. As he signs at book parties. His gaze fond. Unfocused. As through a mist dimly. Bloom is all doubled-up. Fists. *He'll* bang you to attention. Bloom's prose. Two-hundred pounds of metal money dropped from a great height into a Yale seminar wastebasket. Bullseye! Bull*shit*. Vendler and Bloom. Ashbery and Ammons. Ammons's verse? A half-shaved chin. Some hairs left in place. Recalling what's basic. Truly American. Real Southern. Leave the field half plowed.

Bloom and Vendler. Ammons and Ashbery. Ashbery gets lots of lots. For little. Or nothing. In the boondocks. Of Brooklyn College. His tithe to society. Society's tithe to him? A MacArthur Award. Almost a million bucks. When prorated. The promotion. The publicity. Ashbery figures that way. He began as a publicist. Before Paris (1955). Bloom pictured Ashbery's bank book. He deleted Ashbery from his stump speech. Excised him from the catechism. Pushed him farther down the deconstructing ladder at Yale. Enough is enough. Bloom made Ammons his main dummy. A harmless oaf. Not a self-promoter. Not an Ashbery. Not a threat to his cash register. It's the critic's turn. And who's the critic? You guessed it. Anyway. Ammons. Not Ashbery. Number one.

Not for Vendler. She stamped her foot. Could afford to be contrary now. Bloom schmoom. She'd stick with Ashbery. Ashbery remained her critical desk-set. At Harvard-Heidelberg. Just right. An elegant cipher. That's where she came in. Give him syntax. Make him relevant. Plenty to explicate. Mirrors. Facing mirrors. Facing mirrors. Much poetic repetition. For her own verbal aerobics. Plenty of room. For the limp. Lazy. Loops of her. Elliptical prose. It doesn't do. Much of anything. Either. Her prose. Sort of runs in place. An ideal reflection. Of

Ashbery's reflections. On his own reflection. This is wonderful. His existential interfaces. She can talk. About them. Forever. Without saying. Anything. In high-priced pieces. In the big mags. And then the triannual Big Book. And she *does* have her classes. Those kids are wonderful. The way they want to understand the very best that's being written today. And spoken. Talk. Talk. For her classes. Page. Page. For her books. Oh. The boyish Ashbery. Nothing. Like. Him. Ever. My. New. Wardrobe. Wonder. If. He. Would. Like. It?

So the state of American letters had been distorted into incredible caricature. But how can it be dealt with, even described for the world? The literary paralysis has spread to the communication arts. There is no place in society today for a literary satirist, for a Lewis Carroll, an Edward Lear or a Max Beerbohm, the kind of comedic craftsman who came forth late in the last century or early in this one to set things straight when such literary matters got so far out of hand. Our mainstream newspapers and magazines have been stunned and confused by the new literature. They ignore it. Or if not, treat it as faintly newsworthy, an exotic sidelight to more serious matters, like a report on a dying ritual in Tibet, a sign of the times for a vanishing culture. The few remaining magazines within the contracting small press movement either embrace the new state of literary affairs or are so humiliated they elect to ignore it.

There are, nonetheless, many who are truly concerned. They have been effectively shunted aside. My own personal sense of this has been shaped into my being over the last two decades. My contempt has been smoothed over — like sand beneath the tidal wave — to comparative resignation. Yet my lifetime interest in history and poetics persists. I confront the effects of literary postmodernism at every turn.

It made writing *Old Soldiers,* the research, the composition, the publishing of it, a total of four years, seem a quixotic nightmare unredeemed by any turns of whimsy or comic relief. I have ceased to write poetry. Bloom, Vendler, Ammons and Ashbery — and the many new groupies of their kind — still challenge my attention. The cancer of the New Writing has metastasized throughout every institution of society. The decline of formal, objective poetry and criticism has abetted the misuse of language throughout the entire culture. In the public sphere, it has resulted in a devastating neglect of the truth. People are so overwhelmed by wave after wave of hyped-up visual and acoustic effects from the mass news and entertainment media, they can no longer perceive the Babel-like breakdown in communication at the communal level. This can be traced through the deafening high of the truly doomed Woodstock Generation (1969) up to and through the Presidential election of 1988, which dooms the rest of us. For in our current or recent political life, we find the "misreadings" of Bloom and Vendler all-pervasive. The separation of language from accepted meaning in politics is at least parallel, often identical to that achieved by the academic Deconstructionists. The familiar strategies of politicians also share much with those of the Neo-Existential poetry of Ammons and Ashbery, in for instance their attempt to induce a kind of amnesia to separate society from its sensible past and a predictable future—in other words, from history.

Every historical abuse or outrage, in one sense, can be traced to a derangement of ideation caused by a confusion of linguistic meaning (Bloom's "misreading," of course). The swift eye of thought travelling from the Inquisition in the fifteenth century ("Heretic!") to the Third Reich in the twentieth ("Red!" "Jew!") discerns no exception to this sweeping thesis. How will this same high-flying optical orb look down upon America's most recent election, which swung mainly, our pundits tell us retrospectively, upon Bush's linking Dukakis with "the 'L' word"?

Think for a moment how far we have fallen. How dissolute our public dialogue has become! It used to take tough, hard language to besmirch a political opponent. Back in the 1920s (the Palmer Raids) the inflammatory word "Red" had to be enlisted to accomplish an equivalent tarring effect. And in the early 1950s (the so-called McCarthy era), the hiss and sneer of "Commie!"—again suggesting collusion with a foreign enemy—was still necessary for the bending of great masses of people toward hysterical distortions. Today, however, we see the same result attained through the delicate shorthand of "the 'L' word," or "liberal," to dispatch a candidate to ultimate oblivion. "Liberal," no less, or, rather, no more.

"Liberal" suggests no menace from a foreign power. Think of it, that once benign, almost jolly word generically denoting generosity and tolerance, a term of near-endearment in the days of egghead Adlai, that ploughshare of a word, has now been converted to a sword. Airiness of linguistic meaning becomes directly proportional to the weight of the impending injustice. Derangement of the scales of justice once called for a heavy hand. Today, the same severe dislocation can be effected by a light touch of the little finger, the "pinkie" (as it were).

If the balance is finally wrecked beyond repair, Deconstruction in the literary arts will have played its part. Oh, not a heavy part, the Deconstructionists will shrug. In such a delicate balance as our democracy, the part does not have to be heavy to be damaging — every little bit hurts!

Those who came before us, who so carefully preserved and handed down to us our present bounty, our Founding Fathers — if you will, and I must — insisted in all they spoke and wrote upon hard, clear, exact language to preserve the chiselled edge of meaning against all conceivable "misreadings," whether Bloomian, Vendlerian, Ammonsian or Ashberian.

Even semantics, in its early incarnations after the Second World War, looked upon its role as somehow serving such ancient and traditional efficacies. Now, of course, semantics has been deconstructed to semiotics, and semiotics to semiology and semiology to God-knows-what. I can only guess how many college departments have been fabricated to serve the many degrees and stages of these various fatuities. The faculties within literary Deconstruction exist beyond all admonitory suasions or sensible controls.

Our new breed of sophists — Deconstructionists all — will no doubt assure you that learning and language have always been far removed from public or political life. This, too, is a case of hypocrisy so compulsively self-serving that it no longer credits the public sphere and its seamless unity with the political. Using a simple metaphor as a handy visual aid, let's say the burbling springs and purling streams of Deconstruction on our nation's campuses by their aggregation in the mind-set of an entire generation swell and broaden as they pass through the public domain and reach a floodtide in the outpourings of our national representatives.

This is the gist of the argument that will historically buttress and justify the present contention that our politics today are more destructive and dishonest than at any time in our history. Through such ramifying, tributary interconnections, the flow of all this criticism and poetry devoid of any meaning, of all belief, induces and confirms at one and the same time the dissolute vacuity of our national political life.

Obviously, I am no adept, no specialist in the business of "signifiers" and "signs" or any of the other academic signal flags of linguistic Deconstruction. When I realized philosophy had long ago degenerated from any serious moral or social purpose into Logical Positivism, I quit the formal study of it even before it reduced itself to the arrogant absurdities and quaint paradoxes inherent in parlor mathematics. I had already studied mathematics through high school algebra to a quick-step course in college calculus. My favorite and easiest studies were in physics. I regarded all science for what it could do. But this close regard also told me what it could not do. As a military aerial navigator during the Second World War I got as close to the "meaning" of science when it is practiced in a moral vacuum as I ever want to get again, when our bombs were dropped on Hiroshima and Nagasaki.

So now as scientism works its further amoral depredations upon the humanities — especially as Deconstruction in the literary arts — I flash these credentials so you will know my reasons for inveighing against it and the nature of my warning. So you will know why I resist the prevailing view of criticism and poetry as merely playful exercises remote from history. Why I insist that words constitute the substance of our selves as human beings and, therefore, of our very souls, which when raised to the highest exponent in both kind and quantity compound to the nature of our national character.

So, then, words are action. Our deconstructed attitudes may forget or ignore this. But that in no way will alter actuality. True poets like Dylan Thomas cut right through to the controlling moral nature of language as action. He renders this fact as schematically clear as a blueprint for a bomb in *The Hand That Signed the Paper.* An excerpt:

> The hand that signed the paper felled a city;
> Five sovereign fingers taxed the breath,
> Doubled the globe of dead and halved a country;
> These five kings did a king to death.
>
> The mighty hand leads to a sloping shoulder,
> The finger joints are cramped with chalk;
> A goose's quill has put an end to murder
> That put an end to talk.
>
> The hand that signed the treaty bred a fever,
> And famine grew, and locusts came;
> Great is the hand that holds dominion over
> Man by a scribbled name.

To deconstruct or otherwise deny or obscure what is written or spoken is to frustrate the gesture of another human being, and, in effect, the thrust of his soul. Deconstruction does not simply brutalize a person, it destroys him altogether. No wonder, then, that Deconstruction, whatever form or name it may assume, must confine itself within college walls. This undertaking, like any other kind of institutional conspiracy—that of a prison or of a national political structure—cannot bear the light of public scrutiny.

Chapter III. Bloom Empties All of Eliot's Anglican Jars and Refills Them with the Kabbalah.

T. S. Eliot in *Four Quartets* documents his own lifelong experience of words slipping out of focus, inviting misunderstanding. The poet regarded this potential for misunderstanding as a kind of immorality. He did not want to encourage it by any imprecision of diction on his part:

> Words strain,
> Crack and sometimes break, under the burden,
> Under the tension, slip, slide, perish,
> Decay with imprecision, will not stay in place,
> Will not stay still.
>
> —*Four Quartets, Burnt Norton.*

As we see, Eliot worked desperately to discourage misunderstanding in his last decades by the exactitude of his language and the strict order of his reasoning, *especially in his criticism.* It is difficult to imagine what Eliot would have thought of Bloom and Vendler (being linked with the putty-pated Vendler irks the elitist Bloom no end, so let's do it) and Ashbery and Ammons (ditto with Ashbery apropos Ammons), with all of whom the fundamental literary premise is the amorphous nature of language whereby it can mean anything the *Überleser* says it means. In any case, Eliot would not, I am certain, say anything about Deconstructionism and Neo-Existential poetry. The mention of Bloom's name might perhaps prompt the lifting of *one* eyebrow and the convolution of *one* side of his mouth in a wince that could be construed as a wry grin. As for Ashbery, Eliot would protest he had never heard of him. Remember: when someone asked Eliot what he thought of his competition, he responded, "There isn't any." This could be taken in two ways, the more benign being that poets do not compete; the more onerous, that no poet *could* compete with him.

Let's go further and try to imagine how Eliot would react to Bloom's insistence that we all join him in his "misreadings." Eliot, I think, would look upon this as akin to an invitation to a gang-bang. Even a person who holds no brief for Eliot's puritanical triptych of "Royalism, Classicism and Anglicanism," when faced with Deconstruction and Neo-neo-neo–Existential poetry might run for the shelter of Eliot's Blue Rock. For indeed the Bloomian and Ashberian sensibility presents itself as a form of carefully programmed madness creating havoc in the name of novelty, bulldozing aside all the structures of literary tradition to clear the way for the yuppie exegetes in academia climbing toward power, control and cold cash.

Any poet or scholar who is not an initiate in Deconstructionist criticism or Neo-Existential poetry can only regard such developments as a complete breakdown in the character or personality of the national culture. Any outsider entering here could indeed "lose all hope." Or as I said in Chapter I, "reading Bloom (and Ashbery) can be dangerous to your sensibility. . . ." Cracking their books, you inevitably enter a science fiction landscape where the familiar is a form of contagion bent upon your conversion to the view that language has no fixed meaning. For, in fact, we have before us and around us a deranged literary world where the intention of the practitioners is to eradicate all recognizable aesthetic, ethical and, finally, historical content.

So, as futile as it may seem, we are bound, obligated perhaps, to find our way back through the various twists and turns of history that have led to our current condition. In doing so, we encounter Eliot's person fumbling his own way through the tangled past to the point where, he tells us as our best guide, sense began to leak out of poetry, where verse began the surrender of its meaning, and hence of its social significance, leading to the vacuum that troubles us today more than three centuries later.

Eliot felt that the absence of an integrated poetic sensibility in the twentieth century was a kind of plague. He devoted his entire professional career, from the beginning of World War I to the end of his own life (1965), to trying to locate the source and nature of the disintegration in his criticism, and trying to repair it in his poetry. He finally realized that the source of the dissolution lay within the subtle and complex forces of history itself. These are almost geologic in their remoteness. In his poetry, they are overlaid and obscured by Eliot's poetic distractions. In his criticism, however, he deals with the corruption more exclusively and effectively. Though he never isolates it completely, he places the historic break in the decades bracketing the end of the sixteenth century and the first half of the seventeenth, citing both John Donne and Andrew Marvell as exemplars of the complete poetic response that has since been lost:

> ... The difference is not a simple difference of degree between poets. It is something which had happened to the mind of England between the time of Donne or Lord Herbert of Cherbury and the time of Tennyson and Browning; it is the difference between the intellectual poet and the reflective poet. Tennyson and Browning are poets and they think, but they do not *feel their thought as immediately as the odour of a rose. A thought to Donne was an experience; it modified his sensibility* ... [italics added].
>
> We may express the difference by the following theory: The poets of the seventeenth century, the successors of the dramatists of the sixteenth, possessed a mechanism of sensibility which could devour any kind of experience.... In the seventeenth century a dissociation of sensibility set in, from which we have never recovered; and this dissociation, as is natural, was aggravated by the influence of the two most powerful poets of the century, Milton and Dryden. Each of these men performed certain poetic functions so magnificently well that the magnitude of the effect concealed the absence of others. The language ... in some respects improved.... But while the language became more refined, the feeling became more crude....
>
> The second effect of the influence of Milton and Dryden followed from the first, and was therefore slow in manifestation. The sentimental age began early in the eighteenth century and continued. The poets revolted against the ratiocinative, the descriptive; they thought and felt by fits, unbalanced; they reflected. In one or two passages of Shelley's *Triumph of Life,* in the second *Hyperion* there are traces of a struggle toward unification of sensibility. But Keats and Shelley died, and Tennyson and Browning ruminated [*The Metaphysical Poets,* 1921].

Eliot's intention was to bring forward more thoroughly this earlier tough, "unified" poetry as a counterpoise to the overwrought Romanticism of the first half of our own century. My own purpose, in a perhaps too abject parallel, is to bring Eliot into closer focus in light of the horrible developments since his death in the persons of Bloom and Ammons and Vendler and Ashbery. In trying to do this I may be just reflecting Eliot's confusion, perhaps compounding it and not simplifying it as I intended. Even so, evanescent as it may be, the missing factor in modern poetry has to do with the difference between the *metaphysical* and the current notions of the *spiritual*. The metaphysical connotes the seamless unity between the physical and supernal, whereas the "spiritual" represents the sublime unburdened by its grounding in mortal matters. Postmodernist poetry in its aspiration to the appearance of "sublimity" may be exotic but is, in no sense, truly spiritual, not even in the confusions possible within that word. And it has wandered further from the metaphysical than a storefront palm reader, to become a cool, smooth commercial hustle. To try to sort it out beyond this would be to wander past all hope of sensible transmission, as Eliot, devoutly helpful in this respect as well, warns us finally (1945), two and a half decades after his initial observation (1921), and more than four decades before its reconsideration here (1990):

> I believe that the general affirmation represented by the phrase "dissociation of sensibility" (one of the two or three phrases of my coinage — like "objective correlative" — which have had a success in the world astonishing to their author) retains some validity; but I now incline to agree with Dr. Tillyard that to lay the burden on the shoulders of Milton and Dryden was a mistake. If such a dissociation did take place, I suspect the causes are too complex and profound to justify our accounting for the change in terms of literary criticism. All we can say is, something like this did happen; that it had something to do with the Civil War [England's — The Reformation]; that it would even be unwise to say it was caused by the Civil War, but that it is a consequence of the same causes which brought the Civil War; that we must seek the causes in Europe, not in England alone; and for what these causes were, we may dig and dig until we get to a depth at which words and concepts fail us [*Milton II*, 1945].

Central to all this is the notion of "wit." Again, Eliot isolates this in the literature from Donne through Marvell. And his analysis of it leads us to a fuller sense of what is missing from Neo-Existential poetry *and* Deconstructionist criticism today:

> . . . The fact that of all of Marvell's verse, which is itself not a great quantity, the really valuable part consists of a very few poems indicates that the unknown quality of which we speak is probably a literary rather than a personal quality; or, more truly, that it is a quality of a civilization, of a traditional habit of life. A poet like Donne, or like Baudelaire or Laforgue, may almost be considered the inventor of an attitude, a system of feeling or of morals. Donne is difficult to analyse; what appears at one time a curious personal point

of view may at another time appear rather the precise concentration of a kind of feeling diffused in the air about him. Donne and his shroud, the shroud and his motive for wearing it, are inseparable, but they are not the same thing. The seventeenth century sometimes seems for more than a moment to gather up and to digest into its art all the experience of the human mind which (from the same point of view) the later centuries seem to have been partly engaged in repudiating. But Donne would have been an individual at any time and place; Marvell's best verse is the product of European, that is to say Latin, culture. Out of that high style developed from Marlowe through Jonson (for Shakespeare does not lend himself to these genealogies) the Seventeenth Century separated two qualities: wit and magniloquence. Neither is as simple or as apprehensible as its name seems to imply . . . [*Andrew Marvell,* 1921].

Eliot, despite a lifetime of effort, could not define "wit" as the main point upon which an integrated sensibility turns (but he has fed our thought). Indeed, he did not even finally pursue the two poetic streams that flowed from the division of Shakespeare's poetic world through Milton and Dryden. He found all this precious hair-splitting too remote from the urgencies of the last two decades of his life. There is still something haunting and compelling about Eliot's analysis of the "schism in sensibility," a mere hairline crack in the mid-seventeenth century, a multiple, seemingly irreparable fracture today. We might say, as manifested in the poetry of Ashbery and Ammons, a pulverization beyond conceivable restoration.

Ezra Pound was a master showman, impresario, literary producer. He understood the right moment in time to introduce exactly *what* to that particular *whom* in the way of the widest and most vulnerable audience. Consider his own self-display when he invaded Europe (in 1908). His wild tangled hair, his disdainfully pointed red beard. His cape, broad-brimmed hat and widely swinging cane as he swept into London's fuming literary enclaves. He had in tow a tall, gangling gal from Philadelphia (where they invented the ideal of "straitlaced" back in Ben Franklin's day) named Hilda Doolittle. Pound's slashing flair had gotten them both virtually ostracized in Philly and so forced into exile. Hilda's old man was an astronomer-professor. That wasn't so bad. Trouble was, he was more strict and unbending than the big telescopes he used. One night he caught this madman (Pound) flopping all over his daughter on the living-room couch. She was fresh out of her teens (21) and blushed at the merest contact with a male's trouser leg. Having been caught as she was (if not in the act, "almost," as she wrote in her autobiography years later),

she never completely recovered. But Pound relished the wrath of the
"Quaker Oafs." He was really just a big kid (22) himself. And had
bumbled his way from Idaho (where he spent his infancy) through an
adolescence and early manhood mostly on the East Coast energized
by such antipathies. Hilda was nuts about him. So, when Pound in-
duced her to come to Europe (1911), she became his first poetic invention. She had with her a few poems, in this manner:

Heat

O wind, rend open the heat,
cut apart the heat,
rend it to tatters.

Fruit cannot drop
through this thick air—
fruit cannot fall into heat
that presses up and blunts
the points of pears
and rounds the grapes.

Cut the heat—
plough through it,
turning it on either side
of your path.

Hilda was later analyzed by Freud. If the crafty Viennese did not eye
that as one of the hottest poems ever written by any woman since Sappho, then he was not the man I think he was. Anyway, Ezra rescanned
her poems, made a quick incision here, pushed a stitch through
there—and dubbed them "Imagisme." Just like that! But who the hell
would ever publish poems by someone named Hilda Doolittle? He
performed the final excision, signing her poems simply "H. D." And
both *Imagism* and H. D. were launched, like bricks through the windows of literary convention. The world gasped!

If Pound could do that for Hilda, who finally shied away from the
vortex that swirled at his coattails, imagine what he could do for someone like Eliot, who needed him desperately when they first met (August, 1914) to find out who, what and where he really was. Like Joyce,
Pound probably heard the guns of the First World War across the
Channel as so much competing bombast. But Eliot was shattered by
the whole business.

Pound pressed to his bosom Eliot's bitter and vitriolic *persona* (which
Eliot adopted from the French of Laforgue and Baudelaire). But Ezra

regarded Tom's post-*Prufrock* (1915) religious purpose as the death of his poetry. So, when Eliot offered *The Waste Land* for appraisal, Pound yanked as much of the religious stuffing out of it as he could. As biographer Lindall Gordon pricks forth in her sober and absorbing *Eliot's Early Years* (1977):

> When, early in January, 1922, Eliot stopped again in Paris on his way home from the sanitarium, Pound thought badly of "Death by Water." He drew a thick line through the focal "London" fragment in "The Fire Sermon" and cancelled references to churches, St. Mary Woolnoth and Michael Paternoster. What excited Pound's enthusiasm was not Eliot's private hallucinations and hopes but the helpless sense of submission ("deploring action") to the stings of fortune, to London's odour of putrefaction and dull routines. He congratulated Eliot on the outline he had found for their "deformative secretions"....
>
> ... Pound was often ruthless about lines or passages that suggest an imaginative control of the waste. He refused Eliot the authority of St. John the Divine when he bears witness to his generation's muddled efforts to communicate with spirits.... Pound also scratched the prophecy of metamorphosis.... He persuaded Eliot to omit his most penitential fragment, "Exeguy," in which a poet confesses having abused his gift in order to court immediate fame and resolves to carry through the Dantean schema.... Pound, who for years had helped Eliot to Fame, could not see the reason for Eliot's great cry of "DOLOR"....
>
> When Eliot offered *The Waste Land* to the Dial on 20 January, he said it had been three times through the sieve by Pound and himself and should soon be in its final form.... Eliot cut the whole of the fisherman's voyage in response to Pound's numerous cancellations on the typescript copy, though vague doubts lingered as to the effect of this on the poem as a whole.... But the main force of Pound's attack ... was directed against the three closing lyrics of the Lausanne draft: "Song," "Dirge," and "Exeguy".... Pound advised Eliot repeatedly "to abolish 'em altogether".... What Pound called the "superfluities" were cut.

Pound was always all business. He had no truck with sentimentality or long-winded prosiness. Everything to him was ideographic — epigrammatic. If the Romantics saw their lives written in wind and water, Pound saw his chipped in rock. So he never dilated on the role he played in the creation of *The Waste Land,* or, indeed, in the creation of the man and poet the world came to know as T. S. Eliot (up to the mid-1920s). And when Pound gruffly conceded he was "the midwife" of the celebrated poem, he was concealing more than he disclosed, that he was in fact one of the two principals in its gestation. Pound could more truthfully be called the father of *The Waste Land,* who by the active insertion of his own penetrating taste impregnated Eliot's passive material and gave the literary world an altogether new direction. Or rather, a new universe of directions — for this was the time of the advent of Einstein's Relativity. Eliot never denied Pound's contributions. In fact, in later years, he paraded them in the way of repudiation so he could finally move to the "higher ground" of *Ash Wednesday* (1930) and *Four Quartets* (1930s, 40s). Virtually all of the lines in the published *The Waste Land* were Eliot's. But in the original pre–Pound version they were so obscured, overlaid and imbedded in an almost equal amount of dead poetic material that they never would have been singled out for celebrity, and possibly would not even have survived, had it not been for Pound.

Exactly what did Pound do to make *The Waste Land* into something opposite to what Eliot had intended; to turn it into an extended and more intensified *Prufrock,* rather than the kind of metaphysical closure upon religious content that Eliot had wanted it to be? There are problems here. A blackboard and chalk would now come in handy. You can only suggest with visual cues, lines and arrows, the push and pull of the two minds — Pound's and Eliot's — huddled over the original versions of the epic-to-be. Or you can resort to analogy and metaphor. This throws you back upon poetry to explain a poem, an onanistic enterprise. Otherwise, it is absolutely impossible to reproduce the effects of a poem in *mere prose* no matter how far it is extended. Bloom exploits this difficulty, yea! impossibility, turning it into a career and a way of life. That's what I mean when I say that Bloom is the Duns Scotus of our time. If a thing — like finding a prose equivalent to the actual working of a poem — is an absolute impossibility, then how can one prove that someone like Bloom who claims to do this is wrong? By creating a better prose version than Bloom's? That of course would be equally wide of the mark of the poem itself. Talk about the impossibility of proving a negative. In Deconstruction, we have the compounded problem of proving one unprovable negative as being somehow more important than some other unprovable negative. Duns Scotus (1266–1308) turned the entire academic world on its ear with stunts like this. The result was hundreds of scholars seriously debating just how many angels could sit on the head of a pin, as today we have tyros, initiates, exegetes ("ephebes," Bloom has pompously dubbed them) crafting their prose substitutes for landmark poems and submitting them for appraisal as to their inventiveness and ultimate historic value. One guy's guess is as good as another's. How many angels on a pin? Take your pick. Which "misreading" is better? Bloom has left himself one escape: Stronger "misreadings" are better than weaker ones. But that's another matter and has more to do with Bloom's own Oedipal problems (to be kind) than with poetry.

For now the question must be, what *did* Pound do to Eliot's poem? (See T. S. Eliot, *The Waste Land; A Facsimile and Transcript of the Original Drafts Including the Annotations of Ezra Pound,* edited with an introduction by Valerie Eliot, 1971.) Eliot had wanted to convert the negation of *Prufrock* to a positive hortatory religious posture. We are told that Eliot during this period (1916–1921) always carried his copy of Dante. But wait—by means of our own exploratory connections we discover Eliot also carried with him—within his mind—the hymnal-like Protestant poetry that his mother wrote and immersed him in when he was a boy. A lifetime of reading in Dante could not displace Eliot's addiction to his mother's didactic religious verse in traditional quatrains.

So when Eliot moved to convert Prufrock's voice to that of the Saints (Sebastian et al.) his spirit had incorporated, the tone and content were not those of Dante in fourteenth-century Catholic Florence, but those of his mother in nineteenth-century Protestant St. Louis (U.S.A., folks!). The pre–Pound version of *The Waste Land* was loaded with this kind of old-fashioned, conventional poetic mediocrity. "Load every rift with gold," Keats declared. *The Waste Land,* pre–Pound, "sank" (in Pope's sense) with a towering cargo of lead, or with what Pound (who has left us his own legacy of goodly minted coinage) called "dross."

Pound ripped these awful ballads, either religious or bawdy, to shreds, joining "a good modern line" here with another "good modern line" there, possibly stanzas away, discarding all the dead tissue in between, before, after or to either side. The result was not merely an intensified aesthetic, but the smashing of Eliot's original logic, sometimes even his sense and syntax within a narrow passage. The final overall effect was a kind of syncopation where all periodic, classical formality gives way to a jerking, hypnotic, jazz-like rhythm that marked an advance over the static movement of *Prufrock* and made *The Waste Land* the literary *Magna Carta* for the *Jazz Age!*

Under Pound's radical surgery, Eliot's vague, unfocused attempt to repair the "dissociation in sensibility" was ripped stillborn from the early drafts and tossed into the disposal unit. For did not Pound insist:

The Age demanded an image
Of its accelerated grimace,
Something for the modern stage,
Not, at any rate, an Attic grace.

Read that quatrain so that the alternate lines actually rhyme and you will get a sense of the kind of almost insane mocking sound and schizy movement Pound was after. By god, it *was* different — and poetry has never been the same since. Pound sounded a piercing discordant chord that still shatters. But it was not the chord Eliot had tried to reach. That's why he could always intone with too much occultation (mysticism), "That isn't what I meant at all." Eliot's shaking, fumbling, poetically diffuse and irresolute synthesis, in this instance, has completely disappeared. No sooner would Eliot attempt to close the religious gap than Pound would pry it apart again. Eliot knew what Pound was doing and acquiesced in it in the name of Pound's "higher good," the aesthetic integrity of the poem and its success in the literary marketplace.

In the process, Pound perpetuated the metaphysical vacuum that Eliot wanted to eradicate. Ezra eliminated from *The Waste Land* every underpinning of the overview pointing toward a culminating synthesis at the end. The thesis was abbreviated at the beginning, its connectives snipped away in the antithesis at the center, and then abbreviated to the point of inconsequence at the end. Pound's purpose was to raise a universal question that has no immediate answer, whose answer can only be found in the duration of an epoch. The result is to throw all contemporary rational systems into doubt, and, further, to disturb, frustrate and mortify the function of human rationality itself. To put in its place a sense of mystery, which is not the mystery of an unexplained presence, but the mystery resulting from an arbitrary deletion. It is this kind of "mystery" — that of sense deleted, logic denied — carried to the point of endlessly contrived obfuscation that characterizes the poetry of Ashbery and Ammons today, among many lesser lights like Merrill and, yes, even the howling Ginsberg, who confuses thought with noise. All is weightless, airless, unrelational in the void that is poetry today. Pushing off, we float back to criticism and Bloom to remark further that Pound's objective was to make the rationalistic overdetermination of critics such as Bloom a cultural impossibility. Vendler here, in speaking of the rational, is a patent irrelevancy. But Bloom — Pound surely would have run on his sword to think that the discontinuities he introduced into *The Waste*

Land could be construed as having set the stage for the preposterous presumptions of Deconstructionist criticism and the toothless gumminess of Neo-Existential poetry.

This aura of contrived mystery has become the *sine qua non* of postmodern poetry. It establishes the schism, the emptiness, the vacuum that Eliot hoped to eliminate, at the very center of the poetic experience. It represents poetry's final sale (Hurry! Hurry! Hurry!) of its birthright. It also brought about the demise and literal death of virtually all the "traditionalist" (culturally connected) poets caught in its cyclonic suction — Berryman, Lowell, Schwartz, Jarrell, Roethke, Plath, Sexton bore their obsolescence heroically — and then snapped! Possibly feeling erased by the impending new fashion in poetry, they all finally — and foolishly — rubbed themselves out, through either insanity, alcohol or suicide.

What must have haunted these poets — as practitioners of an old and once-honored craft — was the commercial success of the visual arts in the United States. In Calvinist America, money signified Election to the Divine Sphere. These poets, I believe, could not altogether contain their own despair at not being able to attain the same kind of Election and the public adulation and the large quantities of money that sponsored it — so they faltered. A few, however, most notably John Ashbery, having been trained as a promoter of the visual arts, realized that the American marketplace was addicted to visual impressions. So Ashbery crafted his poems exclusively along Abstract Expressionist lines, ushering in Neo-Existential verse, first known as the New York School from the locus of Frank O'Hara, Ashbery's mentor, and the only true innovator among the whole bunch, who, by the way, jokingly called his kind of poetry Personism.

But there's no room in Ashbery for any flippancy about the rich mine he's struck. All the jokes in his poems are on someone else, the main goat remaining his reading public. The effect of all this was to reduce the role of poetry to a very narrow specialty, not dissimilar to glass-blowing or hand-weaving. The only prerequisite of poetics today is the banishment of all communicable intellection. More importantly — at pain of absolute rejection — it must not show any trace of a formulated belief of any kind. Ideally, it should be as strictly figurative as the painting of Miró, diagrammatic like Klee or emblematic like Jasper Johns's "White Flag," "Red Flag," "Target," and so forth. Keeping Johns's "Target" in mind, you can see what Ashbery is after in — oh, excerpting from *Self Portrait* (1975) a stanza from something called *Tenth Symphony* (the title is part of the joke, dummy):

Tenth Symphony

I have not told you
About the riffraff at the boat show.
But seeing the boats coast by
Just now on their truck:
All red and white and blue and red
Prompts me to, wanting to get in your way.

Note the jump in place and perspective in the last line. This is what I mean when I say in Chapter II that Ashbery sees his poetry as the literary equivalent to Einstein's Relativity. He's sure of this, because one of his favorite relatives in his hometown of Sodus, New York, was a physicist (see my own *A Modern Dunciad*). Note also the word "riff-raff" in the second line. He's an unremitting snob, as we might say where I come from. Ashbery is Bloom's second favorite poet.

Moving quickly along, one — just one, please — excerpt from Ammons, more a minimalist, but still Ashbery's twin beneath the blue-jeans. It'll only take a minute. From Ammons's *Providence*:

Providence

To stay
bright as
if just
thought of
earth requires
only that
nothing stay

Here's where Vendler flounces in. This is one of her favorite "teaching poems" at Harvard. I can tell by reading her latest collection of essays in *The Music of What Happens* (1988). That stanza squeezes the very wind out of her. First, she had the flirtatious audacity to turn it into a couplet. Just as a playful experiment for her students, mind you — they love her superficial, pointless approach to poetry. Anyway, she explains the intricate inner workings of Ammons's mind by, you see, getting right into it this way. And finally confesses: "The couplet that I have turned the poem into robs the poem of the doomed *rime riche* of its first and last lines, its form of measure (two words per line), and the wit of the line-breaks ('bright as —' turns out not to be 'bright as day' but 'bright as if,' a curl of thought). My couplet (which of course will not scan either) also loses Ammons's philosophic emphasis on the 'trivial' words 'as,' 'if,' 'just,' 'of,' and 'only'—the sort of words whose insidiousness interested Wittgenstein, too." My god, those kids will be ruined for life!

Just as the center of Neo-Existential poetry is an experiential emptiness, the center of Bloom's Deconstructionist criticism is a final philosophical void. By "final," I mean Bloom *does* allow his favored poets a slice of ontology to work with; that is, he lets them speculate on the thin line between their eye and the sky, so to speak. But he admonishes them, at the pain of excommunication, not to let their view slip over into any other band in the philosophic spectrum that might introduce ethics (morality), sociology, politics or any of the other familiar foundations of the world they inhabit. Society does not exist in the poetry of Ashbery and Ammons, except as it is to be denied any *real* significance. Hence, history is worthless. On the lecture circuit, on the stage or in the classroom, *Bloom* is society. And history? Well, *Ashbery* and *Ammons* and any *poem* they happen to be writing, *they* are history.

The literary world has come to resemble the world of advertising. Poetic and critical principles are promoted by reduction to moronic simplicity and maniacal repetition. Bloom and Vendler and Ammons and Ashbery hound us with their appearances—in one form or forum or another—like Crazy Eddie, Ed McMahon, Oprah Winfrey, Art Linkletter or Phil Rizzuto. Bloom (with a few seeming partners like Vendler, Geoffrey Hartman and the late Paul de Man, to impart the sense of vast legions in a movement) needs poets like Ashbery and Ammons. He must have them as touchstones on the lecture circuit. How else could he bring immediacy to the millions of words he has peddled as to criticism's superiority over poetry? Their poems are so insubstantial and pliable, so devoid of any hard reality, that Bloom's public prose explication of them could not be anything but "strong" and, therefore, more interesting, *per se,* an automatic, ritualistic demonstration of critical supremacy. Put it this way: Neo-Existential poets empty their poems of "meaning" through very clever verbal devices and Deconstructionist critics refill them with "meaningful" prose. Or, more simply, the empty poems are filled with prose—a little back-of-the-wagon trick Bloom learned from the old Gnostics and Kabbalists, whose records call it "the emptying and refilling of the jars." If Bloom did not have the "empty jars" of postmodern poets like Ashbery and Ammons, his fees would disappear. Without the likes of Bloom, so would those of Ashbery and Ammons.

But, to get down to cases, more abhorrent to this new "literature" than society and history is any hint of moral conviction or, need we add, religious content. Even before he consolidated his conquest of the known literary world, Bloom used critic R. P. Blackmur as the crowbar to pry religion loose from poetry once and for all, specifically Blackmur's passing preference for T. S. Eliot over D. H. Lawrence. Back in 1971 in his *Ringers in the Tower,* Bloom, just beginning to swell, flexed to the task in "Lawrence, Eliot, Blackmur and the Tortoise":

> Blackmur is a critic of the rhetorical school of I. A. Richards. The school is spiritually middle-aged to old; it is in the autumn of its emblematic body. Soon it will be dead....
>
> Poetry is the embodiment of a more than rational energy. This truth, basic to Coleridge and Blake, and to Lawrence as their romantic heir, is inimical to Blackmur's "rationally constructed imagination," which he posits throughout his criticism. Eliot's, we are to gather, is a rational imagination, Lawrence's is not. The great mystics, and Eliot as their poetic follower, saw their ultimate vision "within the terms of an orderly insight." But Lawrence did not. Result: "In them, reason was stretched to include disorder and achieved mystery. In Lawrence, the reader is left to supply the reason and the form; for Lawrence only expresses the substance."
>
> The underlying dialectic here is a social one; Blackmur respects a codified vision, an institutionalized insight, more than the imaginative Word of an individual Romantic poet.... In fairness to Blackmur one remembers his insistence that critics are *not* the fathers of a new church....

The thing to note here is Bloom's contempt for "a social dialectic," "a codified vision," and "an institutionalized insight." Even more pointedly, note his apparent agreement with Blackmur's "insistence that critics are *not* the fathers of a new church." As we shall see, that soon comes to depend on whether it is Eliot's church, or Bloom's.

Four years later, Bloom closed his pincers with *A Map of Misreading* (1975), which smashed all poetic orthodoxies (Romanticism, Classicism, etc.), and *Kabbalah and Criticism* (1975 also), which swallowed up all religious orthodoxies (Protestantism, Catholicism, Judaism, etc.). By 1976, he completed his cyclonic eradication of any fixed meaning in literature — and hence of society and history — with *Poetry and Repression* (1976). By 1977, after annexing the whole literary universe, Bloom's attacks become totalitarian in their reckless ferocity. By August, 1977, bearing his destructive bent (called Deconstruction) beyond the literary world to the forums and media of the mass American culture, "in a symposium on overrated and underrated writers in the August number of Esquire," according to Hilton Kramer, who denounced Bloom's outrages in *The New York Times Book Review* (August 21, 1977), Bloom could write:

> Most overrated: T. S. Eliot, *all* of him, verse and prose; the academy, or clerisy, needed him as their defense against their own anxieties or uselessness. His neo–Christianity became their mast, hiding their sense of being forlorn and misplaced. His verse is (mostly) weak; his prose is wholly tendentious.

With this sort of thing, Bloom blasted huge holes in the walls and halls of *academe.* Among those pouring through the new openings was Helen Vendler, now holding down Bloom's Harvard flank in his "open warfare" against orthodox poetry.

Vendler began her career sensibly enough. As she remembers in *Part of Nature, Part of Us* (in the Foreword, 1980): "I had written essays for some years, before, by a lucky chance, I began reviewing: *The Massachusetts Review* annually commissioned someone to consider the year's work in poetry, and in 1966, when I was teaching at Smith, I was asked to take it on. It seemed to me then a windfall, and seems no less to me now...."

Within the chaos and confusion of Deconstruction, Vendler ascended giddily, from Smith to Boston University and, finally, to Harvard. The swift climb has afflicted her with a kind of vertigo. But she has never been dizzy enough to venture very far from her original dependence upon Bloom's strong "misreadings" of history. His dominance made certain new tenets and theories quick tickets to success on campus. Ashbery and Ammons had become unexceptionable as current poetic luminaries. So they soon became Vendler's favorites, too. As for criticism, she only had to switch hands to latch on to Bloom's predilections. T. S. Eliot had during her undergraduate days been an adored idol. She confesses: "When I was seventeen, I caught pneumonia — and thought it no bad bargain — sitting on the floor of Harvard's unheated Memorial Hall, hearing Eliot's lecture piped through from Sanders Theatre...." When Bloom dislodged Eliot at Yale, she caught wind of it quickly in Boston and could write in 1971, despite her adulation only a few years before: "If Eliot is to claim a place in English, it will have to be on the basis of the poems written before 1930. We may all be deceived, even in this, and future ages may discover, as Harold Bloom has mischievously prophesied, that Pound and Eliot are our Cleveland and Cowley" (notoriously rotten literary eggs). Thus Vendler blithely echoes Bloom's line that Eliot and Pound might disappear altogether from the history of literature.

As I say, the new literary judgments are totalitarian. Once you eradicate the past, either nothing or anything can be termed "the true history," as we know from both Hitler and Stalin. Any serious person who came to this conclusion would cease to speak or write of it, out of a minimal regard for the need to function, at least on an animal level. But Vendler is palpably stimulated to insouciant volubility by the Deconstructed condition of knowledge at the university level, literary and otherwise, like a freshet chortling and gurgling under the caresses of a spring thaw.

Bloom is not fun-loving. On the contrary, though he may be "mischievous" in fabricating revisionary texts for his new church, his ulterior motives, his personal ambitions are tough and sober to the point of seeming madness. Along this line, he says with a straight face that he just happened to stumble upon the Kabbalah as the basis for his critical canon (as they say), for all the wacky notions of Belatedness, Anxiety, Misreading, Defensive Warfare and, by implication, the domination of the strongest (read "remotest") in both criticism and poetry. He goes further. He says that he did not realize how closely all this resembled the religious dialectic of the Kabbalah until he had formulated and written such books as *The Anxiety of Influence* (1973) and *A Map of Misreading* (1975). First, what is the Kabbalah? Bloom suggests it's still popular enough out there somewhere to become a plausible replacement for the Old and New Testaments as the basis for Western literature. From *Kabbalah and Criticism* (also 1975!):

> But Kabbalah went out and away from the main course of Jewish religious thought, and uncannily it has survived both Gnosticism and Neoplatonism, in that Kabbalah today retains a popular and apparently perpetual existence.... As I write, the desk in front of me has on it a series of paperback manuals purchased in drugstores and at newsstands, with titles like *Tree of Life, Kabbalah: An Introduction, Kabbalah Today,* and *Understanding the Kabbalah.* There are no competing titles on Gnosticism [its Christian historical parallel] today....

WHAT? You didn't know that? Where the hell have you been? One aspect of his totalitarian bent is his expertise in brainwashing. The first thing in that practice is to establish self-doubt through guilt — You haven't been picking these books up at the drugstore or newsstand? — And you say you're educated? He runs all this by us pretty fast and from then on addresses the Kabbalah as if it has been for years at the top of the bestseller lists, like diet or cat books. Before we go any further with Bloom's "misreading" of the Kabbalah, the alleged basis for all his literary "misreadings," hence for his complete critical canon (Don't ya hate the word "canon," like it should have either a collar or a sizzling fuse?). Here's what the *Britannica* (1911 edition) says about the Kabbalah:

> ... The technical name for the system of Jewish theosophy which played an important role in the Christian Church in the Middle Ages.... While Medieval Scholasticism denied the possibility of knowing anything unattainable by reason, the spirit of the Kabbalah held that the Deity could be realized, and it sought to bridge the gulf.... Thus Kabbalah encouraged an unrestrained emotionalism, rank superstition, an unhealthy asceticism and the employment of artificial means to induce the ecstatic state. This brought moral laxity, a compelling reason for its condemnation by the Jewish orthodoxy and the Chasidim.... [The objections contended that the Kabbalah] was carnivorous, feral, bestial, predatory, usurpative, [constituting] an all-devouring ambition.... [It was said to cause] excessive self-introspection ... [to produce] an individual guided by his own reason [who] became a law unto himself, ignoring the accumulated experience of civilized humanity.... [It claimed for itself] magic ... [and adherents held] the Kabbalah was greater than science to adduce proof of the Divinity....

In *Kabbalah and Criticism,* Bloom repeatedly protested that he did not seek out the Kabbalah as the basis for his new literary church, but that the Kabbalah, like the mountain to Mohamet, had come to him:

> But critics, meaning all readers, must have paradigms, and not just precursors.... In urging a Kabbalistic model, which means ultimately a Gnostic model, I am in danger of appearing to be like those Valentinian mystagogues whom Plotinus so eloquently condemned. My motives, though, are pure enough, and it may be worth remarking that I did not set out upon this enterprise with a Kabbalistic model consciously in view. But it was there nevertheless, as I groped to explain to myself why I had become obsessed with revisionary ratios, and then with tropes and defenses of limitation and substitution.

The Kabbalah is also the source of Bloom's contempt for the "social dialectic," "codified vision," and "institutionalized insight" that characterize much of the criticism and poetry of our immediate literary past. This is what activates his dismissal of "all" of Eliot:

> The great lesson that Kabbalah can teach contemporary interpretation is that meaning in belated texts is always wandering meaning,

even as the belated Jews were a wandering people. Meaning wanders like human tribulation....

... Kabbalah is a doctrine of Exile, a theory of influence made to explain Exile. Exile, in a purely literary context, wanders from the category of space to that of time, and so the Exile becomes belatedness....

And the "Exile" and "belatedness" conduce to "literary warfare":

To see the history of poetry as an endless defensive civil war, indeed a family war, is to see that every idea of history relevant to the history of poetry must be a concept of happening....

He means that your grasp of any idea of what a poem is becomes another poem, the more Kabbalistic, the better. This brings us to his formalization of his notion of "misreading":

I too want to increase the distance between the text and reader [which he also calls "literary exile"], to raise the rhetoricity of the reader's stance, to make the reader more self-consciously belated. How can such a reader make his misreadings more central and so stronger than any other misreader?

But enough for now — except for this: Forty years ago, my aversion to religiosity and Eliot's oblique espousal of it made it almost impossible to discuss his poetry. I had not read his criticism. In the duration of time, of history, including my own, I have read the criticism and found it fascinating. Especially his essays on aesthetics. I still have trouble with the Anglicanism and Royalism. But these are not things to condemn him for. Like anyone else seeing his own death just ahead, Eliot was struggling valiantly to keep his own insides between his ribs and his own intellect between his ears. "To make the best of a bad job — " Was that Eliot or Eugene O'Neill? No matter. All of these men — and, of course, women — share communion in the mind of a person who holds them all — *all* great writers — as somehow superior to himself and the life he leads. This is the true worth of literature.

I get no such replenishment from Bloom. There's not enough to what he says. Taken separately from the conditions that they have perpetrated (like Bloom) or perpetuated (like Ashbery, Ammons and others) or simply confirmed (like poor Vendler), none of these literary people seems venal to me. In light of the social hardships today, of which the deranged literary condition is only a minor cause perhaps, and can be better seen as a major effect, I can forgive the *littérateurs,* but not their failure to face the desperate deficiencies in themselves that prevent them from addressing the ethical failures of our time.

Apart from such failures, most of the people I would satirize are harmless, much more readily objects of humor than scorn. As a single instance, take Bloom — aggrandized, indemnified, rewarded, immured; much more thoroughly pinned down by a "social dialectic" as a powerful public lecturer than Eliot ever was as a literary recluse; much more the captive of a "codified vision" as the great Deconstructionist than Eliot ever was at his bank or as a mere editor at Faber and Faber; much more the product of "an institutionalized insight" as a professor at Yale than Eliot in the belt and garters (or whatever they wear) of his conversion to Anglicanism. Think of the comic paradox of a man like Bloom — thoroughly socialized, codified, institutionalized, so handsomely paid, so heavily burdened with the trappings of university life, so wonderfully cushioned by the William Clyde DeVane professorship — setting forth his Misreadings of the nomadic Kabbalah as the basis for his life's work. Will nothing make you smile?

Chapter IV. Consumerism and Capitalistic Greed Combine to Produce Deconstructionist Criticism and Neo-Existential Poetry.

My acquaintance with Harold Bloom's work would have remained remote and transient had not Harry Smith asked me to buy Bloom's books and describe what I thought of them. I certainly would not have read more than a few pages into any of them, had Harry not proposed some small payment for my efforts. I had been reviewing books by or about physicians for an advertising vehicle called *Medical Tribune* to pay my rent and utilities. When a German news conglomerate gulped up this medical weekly, I simply needed the money I get for each of these essays.

This brings us to the subject of this fourth installment: exactly *why* does Bloom concoct this nonsense? It certainly cannot be due to some wider social obligation. I doubt that any American not engaged in the academic hustle has ever even heard of Bloom, never mind read his books. So why does he do it? And continue to do it with such zeal and energy? The answer is no doubt that it has proved such a lucrative exercise on the campus at Yale. It has been so profitable! Why should he stop? The truth is, he won't. He will keep working the rich vein as long as it yields profits.

More than ten years ago, Gerald Graff, then chairman of the Department of English at Northwestern University, pointed out the enervation of Deconstruction as promulgated by Bloom and his several cohorts at Yale. Writing in Volume 46 (1977) of *The American Scholar,* in an article entitled "Fear and Trembling at Yale," Graff declared:

Most of us do not associate the practice of academic literary criticism with intense suffering. We think of the professor-critic as a man reasonably well paid for a life of teaching classes, reading books and writing books and other articles about them, going abroad with some frequency on summer vacations, etc. . . .

But —

. . . we have little idea of the pain and anxiety, the risk and torment that the serious literary critic has to live with. Some of these critics themselves feel that reading ranks in risk and danger with race-car driving or airplane hijacking. The day may not be far off when no first-rate literary critic will be able to purchase health insurance.

"Anxiety" has become one of the key words of contemporary criticism — along with others such as "risk," "crisis," "ambivalence," "pain," "blindness," and "death." . . . Today's critic . . . in an age of self-absorption . . . may claim his right . . . to let it all hang out . . . to make his agony as a critic the main focus of his criticism. . . . [T]he critic who has surely endured the most punishing literary ordeal is Harold Bloom. . . . [A]s Bloom puts it in *Kabbalah and Criticism*, "Reading is defensive warfare. . . ."

Old stuff to us now perhaps, but still useful as a reminder that we are not altogether alone in our astonishment that Bloom's gibberish has enjoyed so much currency for such a long period of time within its academic confines. And no doubt will continue to do so until people like me, who oppose it, and those vaster legions who support it, find a happier way to earn the rent. Only then will Deconstruction fall back into its self-devised Black Hole of nullity.

This brings us closer to the point. Bloom claims the critic's main and immediate stimulus for his compositions is the "influence" of prior texts. And that this makes him "anxious." And he can only reduce or resolve the anxiety by a prose reaction to the poem that is "stronger" than the poem itself. This is Sophism of the grossest kind. Or, as they might say on the corner where I hang out, so much bullshit. Discernibly, the "influence of prior texts" as a component of the Deconstructionist critic's motivation for his work is so remote as to be, in fact, nothing but a camouflage.

Bloom has a high quotient of bumptious, unsublimated egotism. His impulse to be unique and supreme — the *only* one — in a collegial context has no precedent in *all* of literature. For an informing parallel we must turn to the world of American finance in the nineteenth century. Or to the twentieth-century world of mass media entertainment as exemplified by the phony glitter and mock braggadocio of the multi-

million-dollar arena of men's wrestling. Bloom's sweaty exertions by
the same token have nothing to do with literature beyond his own
claims. They have to do with a need for celebrity in a society grounded
in little or nothing beyond the notion of self-advancement.

With this uppermost in mind, how wonderful it would be if these
new confessional critics — so exacting of their inward experiences, they
would have us think — would introduce into their ever-so-carefully
described "agonies" the detailed progress of their ambitions — for instance, if Bloom would describe the personal circumstances of his pre-
Deconstructionist existence and compare them with those of his post-
Deconstructionist existence. How much money, either directly or
indirectly, has he made from the Deconstructionist enterprise? From
his tenured professorship? From his books? From his lectures? From
his appointment to the William Clyde DeVane Professorship? From
his appearances on various panels and symposia? Would he absent
himself a while from the awful agonies of shuffling index cards to compute and make public the figure of his prodigious earnings? Or at least
approximate them for us? After more than twenty-five years as a
literary entrepreneur, do Bloom's profits run into six figures, as we
might expect judging by the high fees paid such literary stars on the
lecture circuit?

And has this windfall provided him with a more tranquil personal
life? Has it increased his sexual potency? Does he find his students
fonder, more adoring? Has his taste in clothing, food and housing
been rendered accordingly more lavish? Has it compensated for, or in
any way served to mitigate the critical "agonies" he insists upon? Is he,
on the whole, happier than in the struggling, financially modest
perhaps pre–Deconstructionist days? What do his agent and accoun-
tant advise? And, again, do his continuing financial prospects in any
way alleviate the hardships of the awful "warfare" of Deconstructionist
textual misreadings?

After all, Bloom has told us in more than a million words of the
"agonies" of his work. He has put his personal experience right at the
center of his criticism. Why not then balance the personal *anguish* with
equal time for the personal *rewards* and their impact on his day-to-day
existence? Deconstructionist criticism after so many years of describing
itself has exhausted its own revisionary novelty. Could it not gather new
life by introducing specific autobiographical elements as those suggested above? And would it not be getting closer to the real nature of
personal "influence" as the force that shapes the critic's actual existence?

It would be natural and logical to move in that direction. Since the only reality allowed in Deconstruction is limited to the poem's evocations, its resonances in the reader, why not widen this focus to include the impact of the misreading upon the critic's spoils — or, taken in the aggregate, the after-effects of Deconstructionism upon the lifestyle of the Deconstructionist. This would give us a whole new onion to unlayer — peeling after peeling — to carry us through the 1990s.

We can only project the estimated duration of this fad in terms of its actual current and prospective future earnings for our many collegiate entrepreneurs. As to profits for the others, we know that Ashbery, too, has made a fortune, including his MacArthur grant in six figures. Has this mitigated his abhorrence of his fellow human beings? His students? His lovers, if any? Has it affected his way of looking at the world? Or rather, has it worked to introduce any of the hard edges of reality — for instance, toting up the money he has in the bank — into his chimerical verse?

And what about Vendler? How much has she made in the last fifteen years? Does she still gravitate toward thrift shops? Or does she head right for the $300 dress rack in Boston's *boîtes riches?* And Ammons? I don't imagine his meagre renown, despite *his* MacArthur grant, has changed his arid Cracker landscape as much as it has the surroundings of the others — Ammons is not quite so well organized in the strategies of self-advancement as Bloom, Vendler and Ashbery.

In any event, how refreshing, and informative, it would be to have these great literary contemporaries share some of their personal glories with us who have been called upon to bear the burden of their "agonies." And how much more meaningful it would be than the obsessive-compulsive nothingnesses they generate day in, day out for our masochistic perusal. And it would be a relief not only to the reader, it might prove an even greater boon to the critics and poets themselves. Imagine Bloom departing from his apparently hopeless addiction to scholarly cross-references to tell us something like, "Deposited $18,000 in the New Haven bank today — Am shifting $24,000 from stocks to Federal notes and bonds." Or Ashbery, forsaking his supercilious poetic doodles long enough to tell us just how he plans to use that MacArthur grant — a big new house in the Hamptons? Travel abroad? Or a *very* expensive gift to *you-know-who?* Since they are so open and generous, and so self-sacrificial, in their literary exposition, could they not consider the *real* satisfaction that both they and their readers might derive from such forthright disclosures?

Wouldn't the entire enterprise of postmodern literature benefit? Think of the inspiration it might provide to so many of us on welfare, Social Security disability, or nonuniversity incomes. Why begrudge us a few crumbs of hard reality from the ghostly Deconstructionist and Neo-Existential banquet?

Human greed in its purest and most unalloyed state can be found within the professorial ranks on the American college campus. These teachers and scholars — in most cases — sought refuge there out of fear of, or aversion to nonacademic society. They compensate for what can only be called a kind of social cowardice by a secretive and at the same time overblown ambition to outwit and destroy their colleagues. Hence, "publish or perish" readily converts to "obliterate the competition by endless energy and subversive guile."

My first notable contact with this earlier sort of scholarly "warfare" occurred forty-five years ago at Brown University. One of my instructors was a fellow named Bill Elton. Bill had been beaten down at Brown by his own "belatedness," as Bloom would put it. Elton's then somewhat novel analytical theories of poetry, derived from his readings in the later English critics (Empson, Richards et al.), as informed by Freudianism and Marxism, were completely ignored by the traditional annotators in the Brown English Department. These tweedy, seedy dons of scholarship not only ignored Elton but by implication disparaged him for his boyish appearance and its glaring contrast to his grown-up ambitions. Elton bided the moment, quietly toiling away, all the while compiling what he finally launched as his own *A Glossary of the New Criticism* a couple of years later (1948–49) that made him a force to be reckoned with. The New Criticism then inundating the shores of academic scholarship was to bear Elton far forward upon its crest. Incidentally, Deconstruction does not really mark a complete break with the New Criticism, but is in some respects an extension of it, as Gerald Graff insisted in his "Fear and Trembling at Yale":

> I suggested at the outset that the histrionic style in recent Deconstructionist criticism has a precedent in the criticism it sometimes claims to have superseded. The newer New Critics are contrasted with the old New Critics, who are said to have naïvely regarded literary works as static "objects" and to have ignored what we now insist upon — that literature is an open-ended, dynamic "experience" unfolding in the actively collaborating mind of the reader. . . . Critics such as Cleanth Brooks were not unaware that "the modern poet has, for better or for worse, thrown the weight of the responsibility upon the reader. . . ."

Goaded by the inferred slights of his older, entrenched colleagues at Brown, Bill Elton with his "glossary" of New Critical terminology ascended to quick "priority" (a Bloomian word) over his competitors, and, by the way, contributed his plank to the staging more than twenty years later for Deconstruction. Elton's highly analytical language in his compendium owed more to the future and Deconstruction than to the past and the traditional criticism that came before, as this entry under "ontological" indicates (*Poetry* magazine, December, 1948, and January and February, 1949):

> *ontological.* Pertaining to the reality of being within a poem. A favorite term of Ransom's, which he uses to differentiate the subject-matter of poetry from that of prose or scientific discourse; that is, a poem has a unique ontology, an objective status, a reality of being, which distinguish it from other types of discourse.

Anyway, Bill and I had some Brown friends in common, and I would hear about him from time to time back in, let's say, the sixties. But after that he seems to have disappeared into one or the other of New York's huge academic canyons, SUNY, or, more exactly, I think, CUNY, as the world's greatest living expert on King Lear's big toe. He was the consummate scholar.

I was reminded of this about fifteen years ago when I saw Bill sitting with a young woman at a sidewalk café then called O'Henry's at the northwest corner of Sixth Avenue and Fourth Street. He invited me to sit down and join him "in a beer." Bill looked like a chubby little chipmunk, with dark hair, puffy red cheeks and thick glasses. He unabashedly introduced his female companion as being closely related (a "daughter," I seem to remember) to the dean (or some other luminary) in the college where he worked. And if memory serves, they were about to be married (or engaged?).

I toasted his good fortune with the beer he had bought me — Bill always sipped beer sparingly, as if it were something merely to wet the whistle with, or to wash down a doughnut perhaps, but not to be imbibed as an intoxicant for itself alone. So when I, being per usual bereft of funds, suggested Bill might purchase another round, he raised a chubby admonitory finger, and with an impish smile that exposed his bunched front teeth, fended me off, declaring, "I said *one!*" And so he had. I left him joshing with his female companion and chortling to himself, possibly thinking how pathetic it was that I, his garrulous and arrogant former student, had become addicted to beer and all the deprivations that ensued thereof, when he, Bill Elton, knew that success was a much more invigorating intoxicant.

I saw him in passing a few years after that. I was sitting at another sidewalk table on Sixth Avenue and Fourth Street, this one at the *southwest* corner of that notorious intersection. Bill was bustling by, still chortling, seemingly to himself.

"How are you, Dick?" he called out cheerfully without slowing his swift progression. "I read your book!" Bill was referring to my *A Modern Dunciad* (1978).

"Well, gee, sit down a minute and tell me about it," I offered, somewhat pathetically. "I'm buying—"

Bill chuckled back, "No thanks, I don't have time—"

Elton had had a grand time about three decades before, introducing me as one of his students into the *arcana* of the Freudian censor as the stimulus for surreal displacements in poetry, and so forth. The fact that one of his former students—and presumably one of his friends—had just published a long satirical poem (2000-plus lines) and, indeed, had even offered to stand him to a drink in the way of a returned favor, was not a sufficient occasion to pause long enough to observe collegial amenities. Bill's probably still churning along, a brace of books bundled in his arms, toward higher and higher academic reaches. To judge by such successful fellows as Elton and Bloom, a main qualification for the critical enterprise is an unflagging capacity for motion.

T. S. Eliot had spoken of "something in the air" in the time of Andrew Marvell that underwent condensation in the Metaphysical mind of the mid-seventeenth century. What is "in the air" in America right now that condenses and concentrates in the work of Bloom and Ashbery? Mon frère, mon semblable, might we after decades of thought set forth an hypothesis? Is it simplistic to the point of banality to call it greed? Can we make the point more penetrating by describing it as an obsessive covetousness that has no precedent in history, nay, not even in Apocalyptic Biblical times? Might we hammer the point home by asserting that the most powerful addiction in America today is not to sex or to drugs but to *money!* Never has a so-called civilization been so indoctrinated with the love of money, with the absolute adoration of dollar bills, as America in the last quarter of the twentieth century.

I had occasion to consider this diseased condition not long ago when I went home to South County, Rhode Island, and drove to the birthplace of Gilbert Stuart, who painted the portrait of George Washington, you may remember, that stares out at us Mona Lisa–like from the dollar bill. All my life I had passed the sign (near the bridge to Jamestown Island in Narragansett Bay) pointing down a narrow smoothly paved road to Gilbert Stuart's birthplace. This time I made the turn and found myself immediately engulfed by the undisturbed woodlands surrounding the place itself about a mile from the main highway. The day I visited was on a weekend; the log-structured tourist respite was closed; the curator–tour guide was elsewhere, the brochures all locked out of sight. There was not a soul, or the sound of a human voice.

Even in Colonial days, an artist's work could not really sustain him economically. So Stuart also manufactured snuff. Both his red-painted studio-shack and snuff mill had been preserved as National Landmarks. I looked in the windows, too far away to see within. A sign reading "To the Indian Burial Grounds" stood by the mill pond. But I did not move, I just hovered there and listened to the turning of the mill wheel, the water sloshing down from one step to another as it had for more than two centuries. This is what it had been like. How in hell's name had we managed to convert this primeval paradise into the purgatory of grasping, clutching fists that I knew character-ized it now? There could be no appropriate answer — such an answer would suggest a conceivable deliverance of some kind or another — but I considered no such redemption possible within the America I ex-perienced in New York and elsewhere. No doubt I reflected upon Gil-bert Stuart. And upon the Father of Our Country. I exempted them from responsibility for our own corruption of the Colonial ideal, realizing that such an ideal owes more to myth and imagination than to America's political and economic history. By the same mental sleight-of-hand perhaps, I can still condemn Calvin and his mean fanatical materialism for the blight that has finally eaten to the very bone of our nativistic ethos.

I write at a time of international exhilaration at the fall of the Berlin Wall and the crumbling of Communist control within Russia itself and the Balkans; at a time when America is being invoked for emula-tion by the failed East European societies. And I must confess that free enterprise seems by general consensus to have proven itself a most effective and productive component of our Western democracy. Con-trary to many denigrating critiques that have been directed against it during the last seventy years, our controlled capitalism has proven, at least for our time, the most efficient way to harness money to resources.

At the same time, I have remained apprehensive about the resultant intense concentrations of money and political power within the grasp of a very few men with a very narrow social philosophy. For in fact we are paying a high price for our consumer rewards. Conservation of any kind in every area is being ignored; our resources are being squandered on consumer trifles, and our environment is being desecrated. We should be profoundly disturbed by the neglect of the public sphere that capitalism has enforced — the creation of a huge medically uninsured, impoverished and disenfranchised underclass that numbers in the tens of millions. And by the decaying state of our aging national infrastructure, our highways, bridges, waterways and public institutions.

With such deficiencies in mind, who would not be disturbed by the typical American's poorly hidden delight in the misfortune of his former rivals, the Russians and their allies? Should we not fear for an America that can rejoice at the troubles of a former enemy to the point where it fails to perceive its own worsening problems? This country (and its representatives) no longer seems capable of assessing its own predicament and of formulating urgently needed remedies. What, we must ask, will happen when the world economy can no longer absorb our overproduction of goods and armaments? How can our people contain such a contingency without the exercise of a national ethic, without a faith of some sort beyond the lust for money that today stands as our main enduring ancestral value?

Around 1980, I concluded that the two key words during the new decade would turn out to be "basically" and "infrastructure." Since that time the word "basically" has assumed wide currency, so wide that it takes on the work of such idiomatic gestures as "well," "uh," "ahem" and "you see." No conversation can really begin without it. "Basically," we hear everywhere, "I plan to —" or "Basically, this is —." "Basically" has also proved most versatile for its quick and easy conversion to its more colorful and culturally revealing equivalent, "the bottom line." "The bottom line" is usually invoked as a bit of shorthand — a preamble of sorts — to an avowed attack upon the nation's resources, including its population, for personal profit.

And as I also predicted, the word "infrastructure" has achieved some status, a lot of lip service during the 1980s if not much more. But "basically" and "bottom line" have condensed "in the air" all around us to lend an entirely acquisitive thrust to the once-vaunted American myth, making the decade itself best known as the "Reagan 80s," or "the me" or "yuppie" decade. America's manifest destiny seems to have run into a stone wall in Vietnam. Having been thus frustrated, the American *élan* appears to have turned upon our own country for the kind of exploitation it used to direct elsewhere. As the 1990s begin, we can still witness thousands of instances of this every day. We have perfect examples of it in the "insider trading" disclosures down on Wall Street. Or much more dramatically in the savings and loan scandals in Washington where many of our government representatives seem to have profited from what is turning out to be the greatest public rip-off in American history. Law suits emerging from this nationwide plunder will be unfolding throughout the entire 1990s. The losses, edging as I write toward $500 billion, of course, will have to be restored with tax money—an estimated $2,000 for each man, woman and child in the nation.

Traditionally, poets and critics have positioned themselves in history as the keepers of the flame—repositories for the better instincts or richer values of society. The Shelleys and the Hazlitts, let us say, would surely have resisted and denounced the kind of monetary obsession that metastasizes through all we think and do in America today. As personified by Bloom and Ashbery, however, our literary exemplars no longer serve as the vessels that catch and preserve our higher inclinations. Indeed, they no doubt perceive such a function as sentimental and outdated—merely "traditional" and therefore to be scorned.

Ashbery and Bloom would probably admit (announce it with pride among trusted confidantes) that they undertake their respective literary vocations as a kind of entrepreneurship. And hundreds, perhaps thousands, of other academics follow suit. The manufacture of literary artifacts today—as financed by grants, royalties and salaries—is probably as amplitudinously capitalized as, let's say, the production of plastic keychains or Bart Simpson t-shirts. Literature has become a highly lucrative business. To compute its capitalization, we can multiply the number of Deconstructionists and Neo-Existential poets—let's place this figure at a combined total of 5,000—by the salaries of each, which, to make the multiplication simple enough for the poets and critics, we can estimate at a rounded $50,000 annually. Working this out, we arrive at the figure of $250 million as the nation's annual investment in its literary enterprise. Has there ever been anything like it in the entire history of what Dylan Thomas once proudly called his "craft and sullen art"?

Yes, something is definitely "in the air" and without further ado, let us get back to him who has chased it, caught it and gathered it to his bosom as if it were manna from heaven, Harold Bloom himself and his fond, quixotic contention that the Kabbalah should be seriously considered as a viable *replacement* for the Bible, the Talmud and the cultural records of ancient Greece and Rome. As we have recapitulated here, the Kabbalah is the doctrine of exile. It was conceived to be pliable and open-ended, so that it might incorporate the fluid input of wandering tribes forever on the run, either by choice or coercion. It came about when Jews, or Christians in the case of Gnosticism, were either banished or chose to escape from highly structured societies. The distinguishing feature of the Kabbalah and Gnosticism was by definition and historic determination an abhorrence of social structures, of institutions of any kind. This notion of Bloom's that the processes of the Kabbalah can be reintroduced into a completely structured society like that of the United States today invites bewilderment and disbelief.

The presence of both Bloom and his version of the Kabbalah upon the American literary scene signifies the final stage of a cultural dissolution that began decades ago. It marks the furthest penetration of aesthetic corruption that now characterizes *all* the arts, and all the humanities. Contemporary art of every kind, painting, music *and* literature, have been rendered impotent. They lack strength and confidence. You can find evidence of this pervasive *malaise* in any or all of our literary journals today. Even photography — a passive, secondary art to be sure, but as useful as any other as an index to the parlous state of them all — whose tough instrumentality would seem to shield it from the awful subjectivity of postmodernism (that slipshod word again), has been victimized. Hilton Kramer in the May, 1990, issue of *The New Criterion,* in a review of John Szarkowski's "history of photographic pictures," does not fail to note the decline of photography in the context of the wider enfeeblement of all the visual arts (page 5):

> ... When it comes to the contemporary pictures, however, the exhibition goes into something of a nose dive. While certain reasons for this conspicuous drop in aesthetic quality can be adduced from the way Mr. Szarkowski treats this period in his book [*Photography Until Now,* Museum of Modern Art/Bulfinch Press–Little, Brown, 1990] — he speaks, for example, of a sense of "a diminished role for photography, even a kind of disenfranchisement" — what it comes down to,

I think, is the same pattern of decline that has been discernible
elsewhere in the visual arts....

...[H]e says of contemporary photographers that "As with poets
and composers, the relationship between their work and their lives has
become casual and improvisatory....

...[B]ut there is often a case of trying to make bricks without re-
quisite straw. Pictures such as Robert Rauschenberg's, Andy Warhol's and Cindy Sherman's are so fraudulent and crass in the use they
make of the photographic medium that their sheer vulgarity is bound
to capsize whatever company they are made to keep....

By the way, this is the third or fourth time I have quoted—with
admiration—Hilton Kramer in this book. A disclaimer of any kind of
partisanship may be in order: I have never met the man. My repeated
excerpts from his critiques have been occasioned by the perception on
my part that his views seem a perfected and achieved reflection of my
own response to the decay in the state of all the arts over the last
twenty-five years. As a minor journalistic presence at *The New York
Times* (1950–1960, in the Motion Picture News Department) I had
been conditioned to expect little or nothing from its commentaries
upon the various arts. But some ten or fifteen years later (circa 1970?),
I was intrigued by Hilton Kramer's art reviews, which provided a provocative exception to my expectations. Despite the haste of jour-
nalism, Kramer demonstrated a strong grasp, not only of the facts of
a particular exhibit, but of both its aesthetic place within the history
of art and, tangentially, its meaning, its significance in terms of other
arts, including my own interest in the poetic, and, further, of the
larger matrix beyond these of society itself, or that entity called
"American Culture."

So, thereafter, whenever I happened to see Hilton Kramer's byline,
I would literally put other things aside and read what he had to say
simply for the pleasure of the occasion—a rare event in my life as it
turns out. Years passed, and I then discovered Hilton Kramer in the
pages of the otherwise mundane *The New York Observer* (usually on the
front page), which became my main reason for purchasing that
newspaper. Then, in April, 1990, I found Kramer at the top of the
masthead of what was to me a brand-new magazine, *The New Criterion*.
This discovery, too, was unguided by any firsthand knowledge or contact with the critic. In fact, I came upon that magazine in a most
roundabout fashion. I had previously read a review of Roger Kimball's *Tenured Radicals* on Deconstruction on American college campuses in *The New York Times Book Review* (April 22, 1990).

How did I track Roger Kimball down? The *Book Review* advised that the former teacher at Yale University was the managing editor of *The New Criterion* — but what was that? (The name, of course, harked back to T. S. Eliot's *Criterion* magazine, which he edited during the 1920s and 30s.) I called the telephone operator and found it was right here in Manhattan. I then called Roger Kimball, below Kramer (listed simply as "Editor") on the masthead. Kimball was right at his desk where he was supposed to be. The phone conversation went something like this:

Yours Truly: Mr. Kimball, my name is Richard Nason. I've just read Roger Rosenblatt's review of your *Tenured Radicals* in the *Times Book Review*. Could you tell me where I might purchase it? What I am trying to learn is, does it cover the impact of Harold Bloom's Deconstruction in poetics on campuses?

Kimball (paraphrase throughout): Let's see, now . . . Maybe not specifically — but the wider range of Deconstruction in *all* academic disciplines (especially in philosophy and history as I was later to infer).

Yours Truly: Where might I buy the book? (This mostly out of courtesy; to Yale professors, one cannot present oneself as being an angler after favors or gratuities. Such things are the Yale professor's prerogatives and cannot be usurped with impunity.)

Kimball: (Mentioned a couple of stores where he knew his book to be sold).

Yours Truly: How about your magazine — *The New Criterion* — where might I purchase that?

Kimball: Well, where are you?

Yours Truly: In Greenwich Village.

Kimball: Uh, huh, well, I *know* it's carried by the smoke shop at the corner of Eleventh Street and Sixth Avenue.

Yours Truly: That's only a few blocks away. I'll pick it up there. Thanks!

My discovery of *The New Criterion* was a most productive one. It turns out to be a comprehensive primer for much of what I was thinking and writing at the time about the dissolution of tradition and form in all the arts. And it was not only Hilton Kramer who was analyzing and underscoring this decay. Others equally adept at locating the fading pulse of the twentieth-century American sensibility also appeared in its pages. Roger Kimball himself, for example, in the April, 1990, issue, rams home the point that the production of art has been replaced by the production of monographs upon it:

...[F]ashionable artists and critics are drifting farther and farther from any contact with the realm of aesthetic experience, which — despite the noisy cultural vicissitudes and deprecations of the Eighties — remains the true source of art and the gravamen of criticism. What these artists and writers — and increasingly, alas, the public as well — are left with are a series of objects that range from the trivial to the repulsive, accompanied by endless commentaries that present a variety of tried and true political slogans in as pretentious a manner as possible....

Neither belief nor judgment are among the resources available to the "Eighties perspective" that informs the exhibition, since both are presumably discredited relics of a white, Western, patriarchal system of repressive social relations....

In music, too, we find a grievous postmodern vacuity, a loss of confidence in its essentially lyric nature and desperate efforts to hype it up with extramusical effects. Dana Mack, also holding forth in *The New Criterion,* registers disgust with the Metropolitan Opera's (under James Levine) recent production of Wagner's *The Flying Dutchman:*

... But does this explain why, for example, the Dutchman descended what looks to be an industrial crane? Or why the second act, with its famous "Spinning Song," was set in what looks to be a turn-of-the-century SoHo sweat shop with sewing machines substituting for spinning-wheels...?

And as for the humanities, they are the favored and most vulnerable target of academic Deconstruction by Bloom's counterparts in semantics, the semioticists — whoever the hell they are! Roger Kimball, in *Tenured Radicals,* bangs his head against this new movement on our campuses as he encountered it while teaching at Yale. As reviewed by Roger Rosenblatt in *The New York Times Book Review* (April 22, 1990), Kimball's book documents the radical revolution in learning and knowledge that works to wipe out the American past, exactly as Bloom does. Rosenblatt quotes Kimball:

"Our most prestigious liberal arts colleges and universities have installed the entire radical menu at the center of their humanities curriculum." This development represents "a concerted effort to attack the very foundations" of our free society. The student protestors of the 1960s have become the radical professors of today. "My aim," Kimball announces, "is to expose these recent developments ... for what they are: ideologically motivated assaults on the intellectual and moral substance of our culture."

In his review, Rosenblatt writes further:

Wielding war images wherever possible ... Mr. Kimball names his enemies precisely: women's studies, black studies, gay studies as well as the new interpretive studies of semiotics, deconstruction, post-structuralism and the like....

... Chillingly he reports on academic exchanges in which the meekest protests against faddism are shot down as fascist and racist. Stanley Fish, a professor of literature and law at Duke University, pillories Walter Jackson Bate of Harvard, a teacher and literary scholar of monumental reputation [amen] ... for being petty and inhumane because Mr. Bate dared to decry the abandonment of intellectual standards....

Well, you must read *Tenured Radicals* to really believe the nature and extent of the erosion of intellect on our campuses in the wake of Deconstruction in all the academic disciplines. Bloom's response to the wider, other-than-poetic Deconstruction is just what you would expect. Python-like, he attempts to absorb semiotics as somehow subsumed by his own Deconstruction. Here he swallows all the other animals in the jungle to fill a syncretic belly four hundred feet long:

De Man [part of Bloom's chorus at Yale] has re-vivified the Nietz-schean critique of history, applying it to literary modernism in particular, and subtly extending Nietzschean perspectivism so that it becomes a deconstruction of all inside/outside dichotomies that have obscured the study of Romanticism [didn't you know that?]. Rather less interestingly [you bet!], there have been many abortive [naturally] attempts to displace literary history into the reductive categories of linguistics, or the scientism of semiotics. But literary history is itself always misprision, and so is criticism, as a part of literature....

And so on, *ad infinitum.* Don't worry if you don't come away from the above with a clear impression of what in hell's name Bloom is talking about. You're not supposed to. If you feel a sort of suffocation, you have experienced Bloom's intended effect — to smother his critical competitors with the heavy rug of his Teutonic prose! Bloom's main purpose in all he says and writes is to preserve Deconstruction as his own private ground against the encroachments of many, many new forms of Deconstruction in disciplines other than poetry. He cannot tolerate interlopers, such as the semioticists, poaching upon his rich preserve.

In order to thwart the semanticists and semioticists in their drive to isolate the meaning of meaning, Bloom must deny that poetry — which he has expanded to include anything we might think or do — has any fixed meaning that the other disciplines can address. So he goes still further in *Kabbalah and Criticism* (pages 124–5):

> Within the too-large vista of truth/falsehood distinctions we can locate and map the narrower and more poetic area of love/hate relationship, for psychic ambivalence is the natural context in which the reading of poetry takes place....

It might be well to break in here to take a good look at Bloom's sophist maneuvers. I have referred to the Great Deconstructionist many times as the epitome of sophism.

You should read a brief history of these fellows and study how they structured their arguments — not to arrive at some objective truth, but to destroy the character of their opponent — in the case of Socrates, his very person, inducing him to suicide. Study how they make their appeal beyond the heads of the experts or appointed judges to the mob in the galleries, knowing *they* are more responsive to blood and character assassination than to the stringencies of logic. The Sophists will provide you with many clues as to the ways of Bloom's reasoning.

For example, in the sentence quoted above, note how Bloom, having stated he will consider truth and falsehood (of a literary "text" — my God, how I've grown to hate that word), will, without any stated revision, simply talk about something else as if it were the matter in question. In other words, pass from "truth/falsehood" to "love/hate" — The ensuing confusion as to what is really being discussed becomes impossible to untangle. But to continue the quote begun above:

> ... All tropes falsify, and some falsify more than others. But it would be a hopeless quest for criticism to follow philosophy in its benighted meanderings after truth. How can it be the function of criticism to decide the truth/falsehood value of texts, when every reading of a text itself falsifies another?

Satisfied that he has fended off the competitive semioticists by denying any true meaning to language, Bloom, again exemplifying the confounding maneuvers of the Sophists, reverses himself. Since all texts are false, on that basis one cannot be preferred over another. But this introduces our verbose Deconstructionist to a verbal dead-end, and he cannot abide that. Bloom's stock-in-trade is a literary construct that has no beginning or middle, and, most certainly, no end whatsoever — not if he is to continue always to have something to expound upon. So, while it may be true that one text cannot be preferred over another on the basis of their truth or falsehood, we can find a basis for preference in their respective "strengths":

> We do not speak of poems as being more or less useful, or as being right or wrong. A poem is either weak and forgettable, or else strong and so memorable.

Notice how quickly Bloom runs this untelegraphed substitution by us. If he had not, we would see immediately that he has brought back value into his assessment of texts, simply replacing such things as "good" and "true" with "weak" and "strong." In so doing he reintroduces the notions of "good" and "bad" and "true" and "false" into criticism by the back door with his substitution of "strong" for "good" and "weak" for "bad." This is Sophism of the most blatant, fundamental kind.

So, not all misreadings are equal and interchangeable as Bloom has been at pains to persuade us during twenty years, and many books, of labor. No, not at all! By substituting "strong" for "good" and "weak" for "bad," we're pretty much right back where we started in the world of value judgments, where *meaning* is king, *the imperial monitor who will not brook Deconstruction!*

Even though we return to Meaning, as history during the 1990s will surely restore it to the center of our literature, Deconstruction has done great damage, if not in society as a whole, at least upon our college campuses, where, if we are to believe Kimball (and I do), it has made tenure for any but the Deconstructionist radicals all but impossible. But there can be no doubt in the mind of any historically sensible person that Deconstruction and its many branches such as semiotics and all the other flimsy so-called specialties so attractive to those who despise tradition and the past it represents, signify the terminal exhaustion of a culture that began to lose steam after the American Civil War, when the priceless resources of this rich nation fell into the hands of the predatory Protestant few.

As Eliot could trace the schism in the seventeenth century that led to the disintegration of the sensibility that produced Marvell and Donne, so we in the late twentieth century can trace the emptiness of our own time in the persons of Bloom and Ashbery back to the social vacuities initiated by the robber-barons of the mid-nineteenth century. But we must follow that enervating force right up to and through Reagan and Bush. In their Decontrol of the economy we can find Deconstruction in literature as a parallel force that enabled it. Only politicians adept at the Deconstructionist bias toward language as without fixed meaning could have softened up a society to accept Reagan's misusage of the words "Federalist" and "New Deal" that turned their original meaning inside out and upside down. Decontrol of our great institutions — especially of the airlines, the stock exchanges and the savings and loan industry — has produced destructive and murderous social conditions, just as Deconstruction has produced their parallels in language.

But, again, this is the end, the exhaustion of the Post–Colonial American epoch. Deconstruction and semiotics are the indulgences of a cynical and privileged intellectual *élite* that has lost all real contact with the society and culture that sustain it. These empty exercises in signification, Deconstruction and semiotics, are the by-products of a society that has been spiritually atomized by its sanctification of money. They characterize higher learning at a time when its failure to equip our democracy with the conceptual means to understand its own decay and avoid catastrophe is Biblical in its extremity.

For, in fact, we are already living in a society that is illiterate. That minority who can read cannot necessarily conceptualize. The conscientious basis for survival disappeared decades ago. I remember about twenty years ago attending a meeting of P.E.N. at which a panel of literary "experts" was being grilled on what might be done to improve the state of literature in the United States. All the questions, it turned out, finally centered upon the role of publishers and agents — and their percentages and profits — vis-à-vis the earnings of the authors. The vast majority of the underclass — now increasing toward fifty million persons — cannot even write their own names. And these literary mentors are concerned only with their own percentages and profits. Indeed, our Muse is Mammon!

Chapter V. Deconstruction Reaches Its High-Water Mark in 1990, Leaving Much Wreckage and Creating Great Havoc in Every Literary Enclave.

The double-action pump of Harold Bloom's Deconstruction has been pounding away for two decades now, sucking literary tradition from the life of the nation even as it fills the ensuing poetic vacuum with horrible prose. Those who feel that such a development is too remote to warrant their concern might do well to mark the words of Czeslaw Milosz in his Nobel Prize lecture (1980):

> Our Planet [Milosz told an international conclave], which gets smaller every year with its fantastic proliferation of mass media, is witnessing a process that escapes definition, characterized by a refusal to remember. Certainly, the illiterates of past centuries, then an enormous majority of mankind, knew little of the history of their respective countries and their civilization. In the mind of modern illiterates, however, who know how to read and write and even teach in schools and at universities, history is present but blurred, in a state of strange confusion. Molière becomes a contemporary of Napoleon, Voltaire a contemporary of Lenin.
>
> Moreover, events of the last decades, of such primary importance that knowledge or ignorance of them will be decisive for the future of mankind, move away, grow pale, lose all consistency, as if Friedrich Nietzsche's prediction of European nihilism found a literal fulfillment. "The eye of a nihilist," he wrote in 1887, "is unfaithful to his memories: it allows them to drop, to lose their leaves.... And what he does not do for himself, he also does not do for the whole past of mankind: he lets it drop."

While Milosz strenuously contends with the dark angel of historical amnesia as the death of the modern spirit, Bloom with the even greater incisiveness of an easy negativism aids and abets it, indeed insists upon the erasure of the past as a precondition of his own priority. In other words, his Deconstructionism in its denial of fixed meaning in both language and events engineers "nihilism" into the very genes of Western literature.

Bloom and his many followers — "ephebes," he calls them, how quaint and camp-like in its flattery! — splice the virus of "Misreading" right into the nucleus of the literary process, both poetic and critical. The effects of such a perverse stunt are metastasizing throughout every tissue of society. This continues to be the case, though we are for the most part only partially aware of the cancerous invasion. It will take a later generation to trace its ravages upon our own. From time to time, however, we may palpate a suspicious lump here or spot a telltale lesion there. Still, its presence is mostly unperceived even as it ramifies, recalling, if you will indulge me, a notation I made on the subtlety of historical change in general in an early stanza I wrote in "Return to New England" (1959–60), which conveys the sense of it much better than prose:

13

All great events, like life itself, or death,
Or love of those deceased, encompass us
By minor increments and slow degrees
That do not yield to calipers of sense;
But build their truth about us unperceived,
Like dawn's continuum that flows and blends
From blue to blue too subtly, till it floods
With light the careless thresholds of the eye
And steeps the mind in newness unawares
And storms the world with undetected change.

So our world has been stormed with undetected change by the nightmare of Deconstruction. Among the occasions, though, where the Bloomian displacement is obvious to the point of general undeniability was the award in early 1990 of the Pulitzer Prize for Poetry to a volume of prose by Charles Simic, masquerading in the oxymoronic get-up of "prose poems." The disturbing anomaly was appropriately deplored by poet Louis Simpson in an open letter to the Pulitzer Prize board, which stated:

This year a Pulitzer Prize was awarded for a book of "prose poems." No award was made for verse. Does not a rule of the Pulitzer Prizes state that the prize for poetry is to be awarded for a book of verse? Has the rule been changed? If so, readers and writers of verse would like to know why. If it has not been changed, the Board appears to have been irresponsible.

Have you thought of the consequence of awarding the prize for verse to a book of prose? If in the future a publisher submits a book of short stories for the prize in poetry, a book of essays, a "poetic" biography or history, on what ground will you say that it is ineligible?

There are several Pulitzer Prizes for prose. You have taken the one prize that was open to writers of verse and awarded that also to a book of prose. You have, in fact, eliminated the prize for verse.

Why?

The Notes and Comments section of *The New Criterion* magazine, which has served as a diligent chronicle of the ongoing destruction of form and substance of every traditional discipline in all the arts and humanities, both within and without the academy, elaborating upon Louis Simpson's challenge to the Pulitzer board, noted (in June, 1990):

In a letter responding to this complaint, the administrator of the Pulitzer Prizes, Robert C. Christopher, readily acknowledged that Mr. Simpson was entirely correct in saying the Pulitzer Plan for Award states that the prize shall be awarded to "a distinguished volume of verse." Mr. Christopher pointed out, however, that it has been the practice of the Pulitzer board to describe the award as one for poetry rather than for verse, and that "prose poems" have long been a "recognized form." Presumably, Mr. Christopher does not go so far as to claim that prose poems are a recognized form of verse.

He also points out that the Pulitzer board attaches "great weight" to the recommendations of its advisory committee on poetry, which consisted of Helen Vendler, Garrett Hongo and Charles Wright. This committee is reported to have recommended three "finalists" for this year's Pulitzer award, and we may be fairly confident that the two who lost out were represented by volumes of verse.

The resulting decision to by-pass the art of verse in favor of a book of prose cannot be regarded as an innocent one. Everyone who follows these matters knows that the crucial issue in poetry today involves an argument about form — about the use or rejection of metrical structures in the writing of poetry. What has been described in these pages as "metrical illiteracy" has long made a good deal of what passes for American poetry a literary wasteland. That this phenomenon of metrical illiteracy has been tolerated and even encouraged by university writing programs is also well known. By lending its weight to the destructive side of this debate about poetic form, the Pulitzer has not only subverted the provisions of its award for verse but has done considerable harm to the art of poetry. Surely this was not what the Pulitzer Prize was originally intended to do.

Helen Vendler's presence on the advisory committee of the Pulitzer Prize for Verse imparts an added dimension and some validity to a letter to *The Generalist Papers* printed in a supplement to volume 1, number 4. Jim McCartin of Wayne, N.J., wrote: "*The Generalist Papers* arrived today, and it was a special pleasure to see the work on Vendler and Bloom. I'd just written to a friend, a poet who had been done out of a Pulitzer by her. She and Bloom not only are not reliable about poetry, but write such abominable prose. . . ." Those who might feel that Deconstruction is, after all, simply an innocuous tutorial exercise that has no deep impact upon the conditions of literature in America today should be chastised by the continuing evidence that people like Vendler, despite her carefully coiffed stance as a girlish enthusiast for *all* kinds of poetry, does, in fact, play a highly partisan — nay! a highly political — role at Harvard, making sure that Deconstruction is buttressed and confirmed in the literary marketplace. She and Bloom and the others leave nothing to chance. They have been energetically engaged in a twenty-year campaign to eliminate poetry from history even as they teach and write most sanctimoniously in its name.

The egregious instance of the Pulitzer for Poetry going to a book of prose provides fresh evidence, if any more was needed, of the depth and extent of the advance of Deconstruction across the entire American literary landscape. Here we see that it has completely achieved its original objective and finally altogether dislodged poetry from its place of high priority at Columbia University and within its crucial award-giving councils.

Having foreseen this, one can still be astounded by the totality and comparative swiftness and ease of the obliteration. We can only blink, resharpen the pencil and imagine how the eradication of poetry from the centers of learning in New York, the very heart of the American economic empire, as it were, must be factored, multiplied and otherwise reflected in thousands of events large and small throughout hundreds of colleges and their ancillary grant and award bodies across the nation.

One function of Deconstruction's tapeworm-like syncretism is to impotentiate any antithesis to it. Its first point of attack is upon the critical centers of those who might be inclined to contend with it. So, very little — nothing beyond the pages of *The New Criterion* that I know of — has appeared in the way of opposition in the literally thousands of journals that are otherwise equipped to act. So, again, you must permit me to invoke my own early writing upon the tightening nepotism and collusion within both public and private award-giving agencies back in the 1970s that has led to the absence of any antithesis to Deconstruction in 1990.

As a vehicle for this critique I carried Pope's *Dunciad* across three centuries onto the current literary scene in a book-length mock epic entitled *A Modern Dunciad* (1978). Bloom and his Deconstruction appear in later sections of the over 2,000-line poem. The excerpt here, though, shows us how Ashbery and his extended claque throughout the Ivy League indulge in shameless mutual promotion, setting the stage for what has become a complete and exclusionary network of reciprocal support and interdependence beneath the banners of critical Deconstruction and Neo-Existential poetry.

In keeping with Pope's apostrophe, which was itself parodistic of ancient Augustan epics, I address the Goddess Dullness (Pope's invention) and bring her up to date (late in the poem) in naming Ashbery her laureate and Bloom her main handmaiden of sorts. Here, a few lines near the beginning of that proleptic (Bloom's favorite word) epic of mine:

> Remember, I as poet, you as patron [Harry Smith],
> Can't quite escape the grip of that great matron,
> The Goddess Dullness we all hail as mater,
> Who tripped up Pindar, Pound and Walter Pater,
> And placed her offalled paw of failed intent
> Upon the noblest efforts nobly meant;
> Who wrought the strong and weak alike to rage
> And weep to watch her vacuum suck each age;
> Who hounded Dryden, Swift and Master Pope
> To hell and back, and Coleridge to dope;
> Whose presence spell-like on these Spangled Shores,
> This vacuum alters all, good air abhors,
> And Leaves within her vapid, smiling train
> The self-inflicted deaths of Plath and Crane;
> And who may now these plodding strophes precede
> And hobble tropes whose only hope is speed,
> Who though I would confound her still upends
> My purpose with impoverished amends
> That bid you, friend, since poets are forgiven,
> Pin all these faults upon the age we live in!
>
> And, so, forgiven if we do in fact
> Accept this challenge leaving few intact:
> To take our Goddess Dullness' awful measure,
> And risk a finger up her place of treasure —
> Those bards who sow and reap by whom they know

Will match this Divine Dullness blow for blow
And follow any ivied, crannied rut
To tip the till of Yeats' raving slut,
Whose body spray, though labeled "Scent of Honey,"
Is Essence of Y-M-H-A and Money!
From pillow, post to periodical,
Too oddly really for this chronicle,
Those sports who work her carom-cornered trade
Have several heads as hoe, and rake, and spade,
More hats than that, as teacher, critic, poet,
And many funded chairs before we know it;
Anthologies ensue, those grants, awards,
Until, like bulbs in series—how they work it—
They beam as one upon the lecture circuit!

Through such collusion, what was only an ambitious glow in Bloom's eye twenty-five years ago—and a dim reflection in Vendler's—has at last worked to render our literary traditions dating back to before Elizabethan times unrecognizable. Poetry has become today an academic and social nullity though so-called "prose poems" appear in its guise. And as for "prose poems," the French experimented with these more than 125 years ago and found their assays so unproductive as to abandon them. Contemporary American *littérateurs* like Charles Simic have a goat-like appetite for all sorts of gauche literary experiences. We can only guess that they continue to devour the undigestible principles of "prose poetry" out of a constitutional tastelessness, an ignorance of its historical failure and a penchant for any form of forced exoticism. The latter is most evident in their discovery of "the sublime" in the most unpromising places. Ashbery (once a leader in the prose poetry cult, as in most other Neo-Existential matters), for instance, has invoked what Paul Mariani calls his (Ashbery's) "precarious sublime" in company with the Biblical Job in a garbage dump.

Ashbery came forward upon the literary scene (circa 1965) when "literary experimentation" was the main byword. Again, I have written extensively about the fatuity of this kind of experimentation. It testified to the incursion of scientism into modern aesthetics and epistemology, the failure of the postmodern poet's will, and its own futility as experiment *per se,* since it has no stated purpose in its design as to the proof or disproof of anything. Anyway, more than ten years ago I wrote in the pages of Harry Smith's now-defunct *NewsArt:*

> The impulse of most experimental poets to aggrandize themselves
> with the exotic name of a poetic school whether it be as anti-literary

as Existentialism or as occluded as Concretism, reflects the obtuse notion that poetry chronically suffers from too much formalism, when in fact there are periods such as the present when the exact opposite happens to be the case. In the last twenty years, there has been such an addiction to literary experimentation that we have come to the point where the mere fact of the experiment outweighs the poor quality of the results.

Little did I know that these once minor abortive poetic disfigurations would soon become the controlling structures of a new quasiformalism in Neo-Existential poetry.

Looking back, I'm inclined to conclude that Bloom and Vendler, Ammons and Ashbery's eradication of the past and our traditions may not have been the arduous and massive achievement it first superficially seems. Our backwoods mentality, while it has produced a considerable body of fine original literature in Walt Whitman and Mark Twain, for examples, has also produced a disproportionate number of very foolish literary figures, suggesting that the design of the American mentality contains a goodly number of cranial holes drilled there to make sure that ideational outgo will always exceed ideational intake. It is the misfortune of our modernity to be assailed on every side by empty-headed poets, literally hundreds of them. As Eliot said of the seventeenth century, "there is something in the air" that brings them forth, something latent in American history. So, perhaps I do the Deconstructionists and the Neo-Existential poets themselves too much honor when I attribute the removal of all standards mainly to their concerted efforts and not to the more general climate of cultural dissolution that nurtures and sustains them.

Even so, the removal of poetry from current history finds Bloom as busy as Kissinger in every quarter. His latest exercise has been to control Deconstruction in the other-than-literary arts and humanities. He considers Deconstruction of all kinds as somehow his special province. And he confronts every encroachment upon his private preserve. For instance, he belittles attempts by the academic semanticists (dealing with the meaning of language) and their zonked-out brethren, the semioticists (the meaning of meaning) to incorporate literature into their regimens (see Chapter IV).

But Deconstruction is only one element in a much larger historical force (see Chapter III). It is only a minor effect of the vast cultural "nihilism" cited by Milosz. On the higher level, it assumes the form of decontrol in government. In the metaphysical realm, it is characterized by a "scientistic" relativism in ethics and an aggressive cynicism in the exploitation of the human conscience for personal profit (as in *all* the media). Our concern here, however, remains the degeneration of all fixed aesthetic definitions.

Nowhere is this more apparent than in the visual arts. Hilton Kramer in the September, 1990, issue of the same *New Criterion,* in a piece entitled "The Prospect Before Us," describes this situation, again, with a comprehension that obviates any need for elaboration.

> . . . The feeling that the arts have been captured by the enemies of art is more widespread than ever before. So is the sense that the standards that once guided us in matters of artistic accomplishment, intellectual analysis and moral inquiry have now been supplanted by attitudes and ideologies that, in regard to both art and life, are transparently corrupt and corrupting. In the atmosphere of cynicism and opportunism that encloses so many aspects of our culture today, the very idea of stringent judgment and rigorous distinction, without which the life of art and the life of the mind are nothing but a sham, is openly and proudly disavowed. When the concept of quality in art was recently stigmatized in a lengthy article in *The New York Times* as little more than an instrument of racism and repression, the pronouncement of this pernicious doctrine merely confirmed in principle what the new barbarians had already established as a standard practice: the imposition of politics — above all, the politics of race, gender, and multiculturalism — as the only acceptable criterion of value in every realm of culture and life. . . .

In the article, however, Kramer refers to the recent debate in Congress over the reauthorization for the National Endowment for the Arts arising from the controversy over the Mapplethorpe photo exhibit. In keeping with Bloom's dictum, everyone seems to be insisting everywhere today that anything verbal or visual can become "text," that is, an aesthetic object, artifact or construct. And by the way, note how we are obliged to use nouns from the visual arts in referring to this condition, still further evidence that poetry and all other verbal structures have been eliminated from any fixed position in the aesthetic realm.

Anyway, as "text," the Mapplethorpe exhibit has brought forth a million words from Deconstructionist-type commentators in the national press and, finally, in the Halls of Congress itself. So as not to become "one of them," though (see the movie *The Body Snatchers*), I will forego restating the position of most members of the small press movement in the United States over the last couple of decades, holding that the entire government arts funding apparatus at both federal and state levels should be dismantled and tossed on the junk heap along with the hundreds of cynical freeloading bureaucrats staffing it. There has been so much collusion and rigged judging in the whole business for so long that it makes the Congress vs. Mapplethorpe dispute a total redundancy.

Even so, this new episode on the national arts scene has managed, again, to bring forth a couple of telling personal recollections touching upon my own bizarre contacts with these granting agencies over the years. For instance, I was once a runner-up in the New York State Council on the Arts competition. That year, a now deceased poet friend, who was a member of one of the awarding committees, told me later that had he known I had applied, he would have ferreted out my submission and made sure I received one of the checks for several thousand dollars that finally went begging within his group.

My unassisted attainment of "runner-up" at the state level emboldened me to apply the following year. I will never forget rushing to the Manhattan offices of the granting agency to personally hand in my bundle of folders just before the deadline hour. Remember? So many copies of this or that, typed just so on this kind of paper, bound in exactly this kind of stiff folder with just this kind of clasp and so forth — a more exacting exercise than the composition of the poems in the first place.

Anyhow, when I finally reached the drop-off point, the battery of bureaucrats, who no doubt received an annual salary at least five times the amount of the grants they were administering, were giggling at the pathetic sight of applicants like me rushing to meet the deadline, realizing, no doubt, that the grants through their own predisposition would be going to their friends and the friends of their friends. I have never experienced such a dispiriting sense of bureaucratic cynicism, such that, to this day, any notion of a grant-in-aid from any source engenders a sense of uproar in my entrails and gives added acceleration to my chronic vertigo. Yes, of course, for the first time in my life, I go beyond that North Carolina leech, Senator Jesse Helms: abolish outright the goddamn National Endowment for the Arts and Inhumanities.

While I'm at it, I should tell you about the time I came closest to receiving a grant. It was through my acquaintance with a young female writer who one year got several of them, two from New York State. This was, she told me, a mistake of the granting agency. Every other year, she said, she received one state grant, but never two at a time. Such was her sense of the rigidity of such bureaucracies that she dared not return one of the grants out of a fear of shortcircuiting the whole process, or at least surely calling the kind of negative attention to herself that might militate against her receiving her regular grant two years hence.

So, one day, during a period at the depth of my debility as a financial paraplegic, hearing of this from the recipient herself over a cup of coffee in Blimpie's, which she chivalrously allowed me to pay for, I suggested she simply give the extra grant to me, since she seemed truly disturbed by the excessive amounts of money at her disposal. This young woman was herself a poet, but my suggestion, which to me had the sleek beauty of a Euclidean proposition, held no poetic appeal for her. In fact, she did not even respond to it. But she was at pains some months later to inform me that she had finally unburdened her conscience by donating the grant to some animal rescue organization, thereby confirming what I had already suspected, that a cat up a tree has a much more realistic expectation of American charity than a poet out on a limb.

Moving right along, we have already noted how Bloom's Deconstruction has punched huge holes in academia through which ungifted amateurs like Helen Vendler have tumbled and, willy-nilly, floated up to places of great power within the university system. And how in recent years the flood-tide has sluiced over the ivied walls and swept across the larger society and there borne equally unqualified commentators to an editorial prominence they never would have otherwise enjoyed. A striking case in point can be found in Cynthia Ozick. Her several books of flimsy, impressionistic, traditional literary criticism had been sequestered in uneventful side eddies of the main critical stream for years.

When Bloom's Deconstruction made such traditional literary commentary even more of a fringe or peripheral enterprise, what was Ozick to do? Just what Helen Vendler did of course—jettison her former critical tenets and cross to the opposite shore of Deconstruction. Bloom the Boatman will help her over. Though his Deconstruction has washed away the familiar literary banks and channels, he still does not have many identifiable active allies. Those writers he has neutralized, for the most part, simply continue their former work in obscurity, or abandon it altogether. We have already noted the few exceptions to this: Bloom's highly vocal but meagre cabal at Yale, his uncounted platoons of dough-faced "ephebes" throughout the national college system, and, of course, his most illustrious, heavily decorated vassal at Harvard, Helen Vendler. To this strange crew, we can now add Cynthia Ozick.

In passing, we might observe that Vendler and Ozick could be regarded as Celestial Twins on a couple of counts. In a long—much too long—piece in *The New Yorker* magazine (November 20, 1989), Ozick deconstructs the leftover shards of T. S. Eliot's once monumental reputation. In doing so, she confesses, just like Vendler (see Chapter III), to a previous long-standing adoration for the literary figure she would now undertake to destroy.

The undertones of Ozick's preface to her Deconstruction of Eliot smack of an earlier sophomoric infatuation. In *The New Yorker* article, she recalls:

> To anyone who was an undergraduate in the forties or the fifties (or possibly even in the first years of the sixties), all that [Eliot's recent comparative obscurity] is inconceivable.... [F]our decades ago ... Eliot ... seemed pure zenith, a colossus.... [T]he young flung themselves through those portals [of his poems]....
>
> It may be embarrassing for us now to look back at that nearly universal obeisance ... especially if we are old enough (as I surely am) to have been part of the wave of adoration.... In my undergraduate years, between *seventeen* and twenty-one [the same life period cited by Vendler] ... Eliot was to me incantation, mournfulness, elegance; he was liquescence, he was staccato, he was quickstep and oar, the hushed moan and the sudden clap. He was lyric shudder and roseburst. He was in brief, poetry incarnate; and poetry was what one lived for....

Unlike Vendler, who can toss Eliot aside as readily as she might an old banana peel, without qualification or a regretful backward glance, Ozick's dismissal of Eliot as an elitist and anti–Semite, breathes heavily against the pull of her own guilt and remorse. She would feign have it both ways, flipping the coin throughout her essay until it comes up heads, when she wants that, or tails, when she wants that. On page 121, she can write that he was "an autocratic, inhibited, depressed, rather narrow-minded and considerably bigoted fake Englishman.... In his person, if not in his poetry, Eliot was, after all, false coinage...." And then on page 124: "As I see it, what appeared important to me at twenty-one is still important; in some respects, I admit to being arrested in the Age of Eliot, a permanent member of its unregenerate...." Her final paragraph is neither heads nor tails, or rather both, balancing on the coin's edge: "For the generation (my own) for whom Eliot was once a god . . . in the wake of the last forty years, it is now our unsparing obligation to disclaim the reactionary Eliot. . . ." These critics, once highly vocal partisans of traditional or "high" literature, have become fully franchised adepts in Deconstruction.

Ozick strives with much nimble double-talk to hold the "high" ground of traditional literary criticism even as she buries both feet firmly in Deconstruction. Of course, this cannot be successfully achieved. In the *New Yorker* piece, we see she has, in fact, become a thoroughgoing Bloomian, underscoring the dismissal of Eliot's work in the American university system, just as Bloom does:

> In the early seventies, it was still possible to uncover, here and there, a tenacious English Department offering a vestigial graduate seminar given over to the study of Eliot. But by the close of the eighties only "The Love Song of J. Alfred Prufrock" appears to have survived the indifference of the schools—as two or three pages in the anthologies, a fleeting assignment for high school seniors and college freshmen. . . . And the mammoth prophetic presence of T. S. Eliot himself—that immortal sovereign rock—the latest generations do not know at all. . . .

Ozick literally confiscates Bloom's terminology, blowing up the meaning of "text" and knocking the air out of such words as "canon," exactly in his manner: "Undoing the canon is the work of a later time—of our own, in fact, when universal assent to a central cultural standard is almost everywhere decried. . . ." And referring to "agreed-on masterworks—what Matthew Arnold [and Eliot] called 'touchstones,'" as "a notion now obsolete beyond imagining. . . ." And joining in the current obliteration of vast literary periods and great tradition as if by fiat. Here, you should note that Ozick postures ostentatiously to distance herself from this radical postmodern revisionism as the work of others. She says, in effect, or will say when challenged, she is simply reporting upon it and has no partiality as to this or that. For instance, she cites Eliot's admonition from "Tradition and the Individual Talent" "that a poet needs to be 'directed by the past.' The historical sense 'compels a man to write not merely with his own generation in his bones, but with a feeling that the whole of the literature of Europe from Homer and within it the whole of the literature of his own country has a simultaneous existence and composes a simultaneous order.'"

Then she scorns it, not in her own name, but by placing the onus on "many literary academics and critics," when she states: "A grand view; a view of grandeur; high art defined—so high that even the sublime Blake fails to meet its measure. It is all immensely elevated and noble—and, given the way many literary academics and critics think now, rare and alien. Aristocratic ideas of this kind, which some might call Eurocentric and obscurantist, no longer engage most literary intellectuals...." Do they engage Cynthia Ozick? Well, as we continue to see, in one way, yes, and in another way, no, depending on whom she's talking to.

The overall thrust of Ozick's critique scores Eliot as a die-hard authoritarian "who despised free-thinking, democracy and secularism...." But the main point of her attack is upon his anti-Semitism and its corollary, "fascism." Ozick regards Eliot's "objective correlative" as a blind, or only so much camouflage for his bigotry. She had earlier promised some "bad news" she would unearth in all of this, and finally does:

> In Eliot himself they have a darker side—the bad news. And the bad news is very bad. The gravity of high art led Eliot to envision a controlling and exclusionary society that could, presumably, supply the conditions to produce such art. These doctrinal tendencies, expressed in 1939 in a little book called *The Idea of a Christian Society*, took Eliot—on the eve of Nazi Germany's ascendancy over Europe—to the very lip of shutting out, through "radical changes," anyone he might consider ineligible for his "Community of Christians." Lamenting "the intolerable position of those who would try to lead a Christian life in a non-Christian world," he was indifferent to the position of those who would try to thrive as a cultural minority within his contemplated Utopia.... He had argued in a lecture six years before that he had "no objection to being called a bigot...." Nine years afterward, when the fight against Germany was won, he published *Notes Toward a Definition of Culture*, again proposing the hegemony of a common religious culture. Here he wrote—at a time when Hitler's ovens were only recently cooled and the meaning of the Final Solution was just dawning—that "the scattering of Jews amongst peoples holding the Christian Faith . . . may have been unfortunate both for these peoples and the Jews themselves," because "the effect may have been to strengthen the illusion that there can be culture without religion."

Finally, on his anti-Semitism, Ozick marshals other quotes, and then concludes by condemning Eliot for not openly deploring "all of the German atrocities" in a series of radio broadcasts to Germany in 1946.

On the face of it, it would seem that Cynthia Ozick is on safe and sure ground when she condemns Eliot for his anti-Semitism. But a quick second thought conveys the conviction that the ground is so safe and sure that it has been thoroughly tamped, tramped and trampled by literally scores of like-minded commentators. No good-thinking or well-meaning critic could take any other position than she does. It might still be worth noting, however, that from all the hundreds of thousands of words Eliot wrote, she has managed to find only a few sentences that might hang him on that score. And we might also observe she has scrupulously omitted at least an equal amount of evidence from his own writing — and the even more copious writing of others — that could be adduced to make the exactly opposite case, such as — only one instance — his continual and considerable efforts to wean the later Pound from his own patently paranoid outbursts in favor of fascism and anti-Semitism.

Hilton Kramer, who, to judge by the terms of endearment in his address to her and the apparent pain with which he undertakes his rebuttal of her *New Yorker* piece in the pages of *The New Criterion* in the February, 1990, issue, has been a close friend of hers. He interposes as an epigraph to his response a quote from Cynthia Ozick's latest collection of essays, *Metaphor and Memory,* and places her squarely and purposively at the very center of the Deconstructionist literary movement:

> A story is a hypothesis [Hilton Kramer quotes her as stating], a tryout of human nature under the impingement of certain given materials; so is an essay. . . . Nearly every essay, like every story, is an experiment, not a credo.
>
> Or, to put it more stringently: an essay, like a story or a novel, is a fiction. . . . What I am repudiating . . . is the inference that . . . an essay is generally anything more than simply another fiction — a short story told in the form of an argument, or a history, or even (once in a very great while) an illumination. But never a tenet.

And Kramer cites below this a further epigraph, this one from Henry James's *The Princess Casamassima* —

> Her performance of the part she had undertaken to play was certainly complete, and everything lay before him but the reason she might have for playing it.

And taking it from there, Kramer launches *his* critique of *her* critique with a solemnity that loses altogether the unintended hilarity of the ambitions of such Deconstructionists as Ozick — such *new* ephebes — to add weight to their reputations by piling the ponderous poundage of Bloom's Teutonic critical apparatus on top of their own flimsy conceptions: "In a season remarkably devoid of literary events capable of causing a stir," Kramer intones, "the ferocious attack on T. S. Eliot mounted in the pages of *The New Yorker* by Cynthia Ozick has come as something of a shock. Its effect has been that of an act of intellectual violence, an act intended to annihilate its object, and it was no doubt for that reason that it so swiftly succeeded in causing the great stir that it has. Here was a polemic of a kind not seen in the literary world for years...."

How Cynthia Ozick must have welcomed the strength and extremity of Kramer's reaction. This kind of response must have been exactly what she devoutly prayed for to call attention to herself, a formerly minor marginal voice in literary quarters, who now — through her new butch Deconstructionist stance in the *New Yorker* piece — had been confirmed as a major literary presence by none other than the redoubtable Hilton Kramer himself. It could only goose the sales of her many critical books — as nothing else has been able to — sharply upward. She had made it at last, simply by falling short of Kramer's expectations for her. Such is the strange perversity of literary fortunes. As to the substance of his response, Kramer, as is his wont in such matters, regarded Ozick's denunciation of Eliot for his racial and political biases, as a further deplorable erosion of aesthetic considerations in current literary judgments:

> The "reverence" for "high art, fostered by *The New Criterion* is," she writes, "now antiquated — or dead." Are we to take her own essay on Eliot, then, with its wholesale rejection of artistic standards and its unremitting assault on Eliot's character, his career, and even his church, as well as his poetry, as an example of what remains alive and enlightened in our culture? Presumably we are, for there is much about Miss Ozick's polemic that has the air of a manifesto — a declaration of principles.
>
> But if we are to take her essay as such an example, then it means that the vitality of our literary culture must now be thought to reside in this lethal combination of biographical analysis and political demolition that Cynthia Ozick has made the basis of her attack on a great poet and a great literary period. It means that literary criteria are to be banished not only from criticism but from literature itself. If we are really henceforth to judge our poets — and indeed all artists — solely by tests of character and politics, examining this writer for the way he treated his wife or that one for the exact degree of his support of a social ideology we can abide, then we will soon find ourselves engaged in an endless purge of the finest talents. It isn't only Eliot (or Pound) who will be found wanting.... William Butler Yeats was more of a fascist than Eliot ever was, and Wallace Stevens no less

anti–Semitic or elitist. Shaw will have to go, and Dostoevski, too. The dossiers will grow fat. . . .

Kramer's rebuke provoked still another response from Ozick. No amount of money could ever purchase this kind of self-promotion for either her or her otherwise unprovocative books of criticism. Her rejoinder to his rejoinder and his further rejoinder to her rejoinder to his rejoinder (isn't this fun?) both appeared in the April, 1990, issue of *The New Criterion*. The new exchange centered upon very nice (mincing, the post–Elizabethans would have said) distinctions in their respective definitions of what Ozick called "our nativistic ethos" and to what degree such a spectrum of values invited, tolerated or rejected Semitism within the American literary mystique. At times the quarrel between Ozick and Kramer demonstrated the smitten bitterness of a lover's spat:

> And right here — on the question of "alien" — you severely disappoint me with an unworthy aside [she fairly snarled] when you speak on page eight of a "Jewish tradition neither indigenous nor widely shared." Not indigenous? Not widely shared? Do you forget our Puritan-Hebraic origins? Do you forget the explicit source of the Fifth Amendment? Do you forget the covenantal theory of a Constitution binding diverse bloodlines through an act of intellectual allegiance to a set of jurisprudential principles? Do you forget the Biblical heritage that is intrinsic to our language and literature? . . . And in the wake of your having dismissed the most venerable pillar of Western culture as "neither indigenous nor widely shared," you charge me with a cultural disavowal tantamount to "an act of intellectual violence"?

Kramer makes so bold as to acknowledge at one point that a kind of "casual social" anti–Semitism was endemic to the New England of his childhood.

> On the question of Jewish tradition, which I described in my essay as "neither indigenous nor widely shared" in American cultural life: You ask me if I have forgotten "our Puritan-Hebraic origins?" I hasten to assure you I have not. I grew up in a small New England town where it was not at all uncommon to encounter teachers and clergymen who, having been educated in the old theological tradition — a tradition, by the way, that owed something to the "island church" [Eliot's] you were concerned to disparage — were as fluent in Hebrew as they were in Greek and Latin. But these learned gentlemen would have been astonished to discover that they had much to do with the observance or even awareness of Jewish tradition in the modern world. Many of them were, in fact, anti–Semitic in the casual social way that was common at the time. It was you, not I, in any case, who

introduced the odious question of "natural tissue" in American
cultural life that might be invoked as the basis for rejecting "Eliot's
'high culture.'"

The description of something as currently loaded as "anti–Semitism" as once "casual and social" must have pumped a fresh stinging
flush to Ozick's cheek. Kramer shows considerable guts in touching
upon — even as lightly as he does — such a subject, with the historic impact of the Holocaust still so immediately bearing down upon us, as
if it occurred only yesterday and not more than forty-five years ago.
It will take at least two more generations to provide the sort of neutral,
nonhysterical ground whereupon Jews and Gentiles might undertake
some more thorough accommodation that would do no violence to the
tenets of either Judaism or Christianity and work to render anything
like the Holocaust a patent prohibitive historical impossibility in the
future.

In coming even this close (not very) to such a subject, I feel a certain
apprehension, a sense of moving too near a very hot stove. As a population at a certain point in time, we have become so sensitized to this
issue that even the most oblique reference to the most trivial question
in this area has the unnerving import of an ominous unpredictable ex-
plosive device.

In fact, the publication of my *A Modern Dunciad* in 1978 brought this
point home to me with emphatic effect. Having read the poem, someone wrote me and called into question two lines that he felt smacked
of anti–Semitism (two lines, by the way, that I cited earlier). The lines
were:

> Whose body spray, though labelled "Scent of Honey,"
> Is Essence of Y-M-H-A and Money!

When I wrote them, I sensed that the coupling of YMHA and money
might be construed by some conceivable reach of the Jewish Defense
League as invoking some ancient Christian stereotype of Jews. I was
so wary of such a misinterpretation that I am ashamed to say that at
one point I thought to rewrite the line so as not to expose it to
something so extraneous to its intended meaning, which was an in-
dictment of *all* modern poets, not Jewish ones, as unmitigated money-
grubbers. I let it stand nonetheless. After all, that was the name of the
place when I went to what is also known as "The 92nd Street Y" to
hear, among others, W. S. Merwin read. I decided that the greater
courage lay in adhering to reportorial exactitude and not in a timorous

hedge to avoid an unwarranted charge of anti–Semitism. But the fact that someone did write wondering where I stood on such a matter, is a good index to the validity of my original (and continuing) apprehensions in this, and to the current public sensitization that could produce such a query in the first place.

Chapter VI. Pinpointing the Many Wheels Within Literature Today as an Initial Approach to Deconstructing Deconstruction.

We are rapidly getting to the point where something must be done to dismantle the vast and evergrowing Deconstructionist literary network. As a first step, let's see just how academic, Neo-Existential poets, critics — and book reviewers — like Paul Mariani — function to keep the public from assessing competing aesthetic systems.

I cited in Chapter V a reference to my own mock epic, *A Modern Dunciad*. Even this brief reference to a poem *per se* — the *Ding-an-sich*, as it were — has somehow fitted out and extended my imagination to aspire to the extravagant ellipses of Shelley's Skylark. *A Modern Dunciad* was a sheer delight to compose back in those happy, careless late 1970s before Deconstruction reared its intrusive head right where the sun was supposed to rise. The merest mention of an actual poem, even in the baleful context of the Ozick-Kramer debate over T. S. Eliot's presumed anti–Semitism, manages somehow to disentangle my mind from the snarls and coils of Deconstruction versus Traditionalism, of High Art versus Pop Art, of Canon versus Text and all the other essentially ultra-academic antipoetic dichotomies that have replaced poetry itself as the central consideration of literature today.

We are by no means finished with Deconstruction. Its sundry pollutants will continue to befoul our cultural atmosphere throughout much of the 1990s. More immediately, I will *have* to return to the dialogue between Ozick and Kramer in *The New Yorker* and *The New Criterion* magazines in a moment, since it so obviously feeds That Great Computer in the Sky that will determine the parameters (as they say) of Post-postmodern criticism throughout the new decade. But first I would like to make so bold as to present you with bits and pieces of recent literary history as cast up in the aftermath of *A Modern Dunciad*. These will include quick Polaroid shots of some of the principals upon the American literary scene today—including, among others, Richard Howard and Paul Mariani—who through reciprocating mutual referrals in lecturing, teaching, publishing and grants maintain absolute and exclusionary control over our highly profitable academic literary industry on a national scale. It may be that their candid and unplanned posturings and peregrinations will prove more informative of the *real* nature of Post-postmodernism between 1970 and the year 2000 than the heavy hermeneutical pontifications of all the Blooms, Vendlers and Ozicks combined.

And you will remember, I *warned* you I might simply nod out if I inhaled too much of Bloom's toxic Teutonic prose: "So if I seem to stray from the field for a moment or two [I wrote at the outset of Chapter II], kindly indulge me. Simply chalk it up to a call of nature or a memory so gouged and gutted by ravines due to shock and gullies due to sheer work ... that it favors the dispersal of fact over its confluence as the quickest way to the mainstream today...." Right now, I have been wandering without much reward in the maze of Bloom's *Map of Misreading* (1975) for almost a year, so long, in fact, that I fear for the worst—that I might personally disappear from this enterprise altogether—just simply evaporate, or turn into a bellybutton full of irreversible dust. So, I *must* divert my dangerously over-exposed gaze from Bloom's searing, radioactive brilliancies—I *must* rejoin the human race by revisiting—at least briefly—the commonplaces ("banalities," Paul Mariani would call them, hoping to accomplish that wizard-like academic critical maneuver whereby the Deconstructionist adepts in our midst get rid of something at the very instant they bring it up) in my own *A Modern Dunciad*.

In requoting a couple of lines from the *Dunciad* within Chapter V, I mentioned my presence in the late 1970s at the YMHA, or the 92nd Street "Y," that major interchange for the Western world's heavy literary freight. As I've stated, W. S. Merwin was reading on the night in question. More important, also in the auditorium was none other than Richard Howard, that globe-trotting and prize-winning literary kibitzer, whose presence at gatherings of this kind has about it the bristling, riveting air of a satellite dish at an emergency session of the United Nations. Anyway, there he was, Richard Howard

himself—right there in the row directly in front of me. To either side
of him were a number of female poetry groupies. Their conversation
before and after the reading suggested they were from nearby Hunter
College.

As it turned out, Merwin's reading moved them greatly. "My god!"
one of the young women gasped, as if from the very verge of hyperven-
tilation. "He's absolutely beautiful! Where does he teach?"

"Teach?!" Richard Howard exclaimed incredulously, aghast at the
merest notion of such a waste of poetic talent. "That man's so *good* he
doesn't *have* to teach!"

This brief exchange, overheard by me that night, gave rise to two
lines in my *Dunciad* that were to outrage Richard Howard when the
book was published two years later:

> And Howard, with his Hunter "groupies" near,
> Said something clever for the crowd to hear—

As general as they are, the lines might have derived some of their
mocking flippancy from my happenstantial encounters with Richard
Howard on several subsequent occasions—for, once I knew who this
guy was, I seemed to see him everywhere. For instance, if I went into
a coffee shop near Gramercy Park, there he might be, nibbling on a
toasted English muffin, declaiming broadly on the rigors of translating
from the French into English; or, should I happen to enter, let's say,
Tony Roma's—behold!—this same literary celebrity might be seen at
one of the booths or tables gnawing on a rack of ribs, telling all and
sundry of his ongoing friendships with the rich and famous, various
decaying celebrities wasting their time at one lush corner of the globe
or another. The Duke and Duchess of Windsor, for instance. On such
public occasions, Richard Howard always seemed surrounded by
small packs of mouse-like poetry enthusiasts hanging on his every
word. So, my satirical couplet was packed, not only with historical immediacy but with an ultimate, judicious ethical balance as well.

Even so, after *A Modern Dunciad* was finally published in 1978 by
Harry Smith, I happened to be on my way to a meeting of P.E.N. at
the Salmagundi Club on Fifth Avenue in Greenwich Village when an
old friend hurried down the steps to defer my arrival.

"Hey listen!" this fellow hastened to warn me. "Richard Howard's
in there. He's seen a copy of your *Dunciad* and's as mad as a hornet.
He acts like he wants to punch you in the nose—." This poetry business can turn out to be dangerous.

I was taken aback by the alert. Within my crusty, combative literary *persona,* there lurks — cowers, I suppose I should confess — a very private, diffident person who has good reason in this and other respects to maintain a low profile. I continued on my way anyhow and entered the meeting, where, sure enough, Richard Howard was much in evidence *per usual.* But the evening proceeded without confrontation between us.

Why Richard Howard was so upset by those two innocuous lines, we may never know, unless he found himself conflicted by contradictory impulses. On the one hand, I think he would have liked to jump to the defense of his many friends I tried to excoriate in the poem. At the same time, I'm sure he felt equally constrained to shun the poem, to ignore it altogether so that it might pass without effect. More about this sort of censorship by silence in a moment. But Richard Howard was flattering himself even in this, his sputtering consternation. He had *no* reason to take my satire so personally. He figures in a small corner of the tapestry I wove — his part, as inconsequential as a scatter-rug at a Fire Island beach house — to expose the nepotism and collusion back then that have prepared the way for the *elitism* and *preciosity* that preside over the world of Post-postmodern literature today.

Another busy, busy beaver at the literary log jam that academic Deconstruction has become, is one Paul Mariani at the University of Massachusetts, who composes flimsy little well-behaved poems as if from spider spit, in the diffident Neo-Existential mode, living the roistering life of the poet only vicariously as in his recent tepidly received biography of the wild and unbridled John Berryman. Where Richard Howard might actually pop up almost anywhere in real life, Mariani's presence is equally omnipervasive, *but* in the pages of the literary press. You could win a good wager at your local bar — and incidentally run the risk of being eyed thereafter as a very strange dude indeed — by betting that at least one poem, review, press notice or letter-to-the-editor by Paul Mariani would appear somewhere in this world during any given seven-day period. Let's try it: Today is Wednesday, October 18, 1990. Here's last week's Sunday *New York Times* — he hits in there all the time. Flip through the latest *Book Review* of Sunday, October 15, the letters-to-the-editor page. Voilà! There he is, bigger than — well, bigger than Richard Howard — in a lengthy carefully glued casuistical construct, admonishing Vivian Gornick not to rough up the prose of Andre Dubus. Right off the bat Mariani lets you know you're up against an academic pro —

To the Editor:

There's a lot of intelligence mixed in with some raging nonsense in Vivian Gornick's essay "Tenderhearted Men: Lonesome, Sad and Blue" (Sept. 16) . . . [Mariani proceeds to cast doubt on Gornick's doubts about Andre Dubus's short story "A Father's Story"].

— by hugging Gornick to his bosom and shoving her away at one and the same time, like a guy who befriends you at the edge of a cliff with an encircling arm, and then proceeds to push you right off!

The other several hundred words in Mariani's letter are irrelevant to our focus. I have cited it only to indicate the kind of energy and ingenuity utilized by academic Post-postmodern critics and poets (Mariani is a good example because he is both) to maintain Deconstruction and Neo-Existentialism at the center of our literary society, how they continue to strengthen their support mechanisms by constant activity on *all* fronts, like the omnipresent Paul Mariani, who with a single stroke (above) ushers one person into the national network (Dubus) and simultaneously ushers another person (Gornick) out of it.

No harm in this, you might think. No evidence of questionable ulterior motives here. *But* you might think wrong. Let the thought keep simmering for a minute; you *might* come to the conclusion that prose writer Andre Dubus is either a close friend of Paul Mariani, or will be very soon. Paul's always greasing up reputations this way. One of the chants around the Maypole that is literary popularity these Deconstructionist days, as we have noticed often in previous chapters, is, "What goes around comes around!"

Paul has won many converts to his causes this way, and he has many causes, and they all have in common only one thing, that they coalesce to the advancement of Paul Mariani, and so of his kind of literature, both within and beyond the campus. His careful correction of Dubus's "errors" seems at first blush so kind, a helping hand over to the proper Post-postmodern path (read today, Deconstruction). Gee, you reflect, he must be quite a nice guy. He's made so many friends. What you may not have right on the tip of your logic is that Vivian Gornick must be an anti–Deconstructionist and a traditionalist, in other words, *not* an important beaver at the dam, so she can be safely nudged aside this way. Still, you think, if you are you and not *me*, this guy Mariani doesn't seem to have a single real enemy in the world. *However,* and this is the main "however" here, there are still other present-day "losers" he can afford to alienate—like myself, for instance. When told that *Parnassus* had assigned my *A Modern*

Dunciad to Paul Mariani for review, I was quite hopeful that at last my book would receive some sort of fair hearing before university audiences, for whom, you should know, it was written in the first place, and who might happen to read a review in a journal like *Parnassus* — back then, anyway, before Deconstruction discouraged such habits.

You see, *A Modern Dunciad* had not received *any* reviews in New York City when it was published in 1978 — none at all! And this was *very* unusual for a book produced so elegantly by The Smith: expensive vellum paper, a new specially designed typeface to convey the patina of an earlier century. I had put a year of research immediately behind the effort and a lifetime (I'm now 65) of continual literary assimilation behind *that*, with almost a full year — full time — to write it, over and over again to get it as exact as I could to serve its several purposes; finally, there was a promotional campaign that went far beyond anything The Smith had done for the scores of other poetry books it had published since its founding in 1964. But no notice whatsoever when my *Dunciad* came out in New York — not a single paragraph. And, as I say, this seemed strange at the time — and remains suspicious, because certain noteworthy New York book editors, like Eliot Fremont-Smith at the *Village Voice,* had made it known they "liked" the book and felt it should be reviewed.

Then the negative reports began to filter back. We heard that both This and That editor had assigned *A Modern Dunciad* for review, but the book was being returned unreviewed. Why? Typical was a note to The Smith from one reviewer for a chain of news outlets in the Northeast. His name should be disclosed only in the event of further challenge to these facts (we have a copy of his note), but disclosure that he wrote such a thing would surely get him fired as a reviewer for the news chain and might even cast suspicion upon his other job as a professor of literature at a university. In any event, this fellow wrote: ". . . Although I chuckled over Richard Nason's *Dunciad,* I would be put in the permanent 'out house' by some of the august Nason chooses to oppose. Yes, the poetry of politics and the politics of poetry is often as fulsome as any corruption we know. I doubt whether [the paper's name] would print it. . . ." There were letters from other reviewers in the same vein.

There also seemed to be strong initial assent from a few daily and weekly literary outlets in New York City. For instance, Eliot Fremont-Smith wrote to me on March 26, 1979: ". . . just to let you know —

belatedly . . . I hope we can have something on *A Modern Dunciad* in the *Voice* ere long. . . ." Finally, direct and indirect word during the next year or so suggested that Fremont-Smith — and possibly others — had assigned the book over and over again but seemed never able to get a review. So when *A Modern Dunciad* was finally assigned by *Parnassus* to Good Guy Paul Mariani, I was elated. After all, as stated, I had written *A Modern Dunciad* for college students. It was designed to serve as a companion-piece to Pope's own *Dunciad* (1727). That's why there were so many footnotes lined up below each page. By superimposing, you could say, my *Dunciad* 250 years later upon Pope's schema, a student might be enabled to experience an interplay between the Classical and Modern poetic eras, bringing forth certain parallels that would at the same time accentuate the shifts and changes in substance and sensibility that cannot be realized, not poetically anyway, in any other way.

Here at last, I had reason to expect, *A Modern Dunciad* would receive the careful attention that could convey the *kind* of book it is — what it tried to do — and to what extent it might serve such a rare and important purpose, especially in light of the fact that nobody since Pope had attempted such a thing on such a scale before. Yes, I had reason to be hopeful. I had never known Paul Mariani to dismiss *any* book of poetry. He most certainly, I thought, would never frustrate through his own contrivances the prospective response of those for whom the book was intended. He would most likely let others judge it for themselves, though he *might* say that it was not, personally, his Neo-Existential cup of tea. Surely as a teacher of Western literary history (or however he might view himself), he must welcome my attempt to revive the ancient spirit of satire in a literary era that is devoid of it. The latter-day Hippie snideness of much Neo-Existential poetry is *not* satire! More of this later as well . . . At that time, I was quite sure that my *Dunciad* would at last find its proper audience and undo the great harm that I knew had ensued from the press blackout in New York City.

How wrong can a guy turn out to be? Very, let me tell you. Mariani's review was such that had any New York editor still been tilting toward a review, it would have reversed his inclination and finally dispatched *A Modern Dunciad* toward the "Out" basket forever. Is that what Mariani intended? *Judge for yourself.* He gets right down to it. His review in the fall/winter, 1982, issue of *Parnassus: Poetry in Review* begins:

Weeks afterwards and the designing eye ["designing"? Good way of putting it!] of the critic is still trying to find a way around five voices so different that it takes a review like *Parnassus* [no doubt about *his* favorite reading matter!] to corner them all into something like the same metaphysical room. Richard Nason especially seems to keep shifting for the door, taking two cocktails with him while he mumbles something under his breath about the goddam ill-bred decadence of all poetry since the death of the good Doctor Sam Johnson. In the back of a copy of his attack on Modern Poetry is a copy of something [get this! "Something," as if it might be a dab of dogshit! It was obviously a "profile" of me as a professional writer and thirty-year inhabitant of the Village; this guy's clever all right, and very careful—I'm sure he was sure at the time, I'd never get a hearing] from the *Village Voice* by Richard Walton about the "continuing conspiracy of silence" in New York surrounding Nason's satire. For if *A Modern Dunciad* has met with a deafening silence on all fronts, Walton suspects, it is because Nason's is such a witty and devastating attack on the literary establishment, which had now crowned John Ashbery King of Dullness. . . .

Is Mariani's review a product of independent thought? Or could it be the remote result of the same collusion — either xeroxed or telegraphed by habits of thought—that prevented *A Modern Dunciad* from being reviewed in New York in the first place? One thing we all must do finally is decide how Neo-Existential poetry maintains its increasingly oppressive, exclusionary hold upon our literary society. Is it really just the age-old cohesion of literary allies in a common cause? Or could it not be something more subtle and insidious, something akin to the self-definition of a caste, or class or private club that engages in practices both open and closed to maintain itself, for all the same reasons or privilege, profit and power—through biases and prejudices based upon *kind,* not *quality,* and through a sort of subterfuge, presenting itself as an open society, when it is, in fact, closed to the uninitiated?

How can we—how can *you*—ever really know? Must we await the hundreds of books during this decade that will be written by apostates and defectors from Post-postmodern poetry programs and networks throughout the country to find out what sort of careful deceptions and misrepresentations are being carried on right now in our own era? Or might we not *anticipate* the deconstruction of Deconstruction itself? — To accelerate it? One way we might do this is compare the review of Paul Mariani, one of its practitioners, with the work of Richard Nason, one of his targets, in the instance of *A Modern Dunciad.* Those who question the objectivity of this as an appropriate proof of a general condition in our World of Letters today should know that I have folders almost two feet thick with advisories from various parts of the country suggesting that I, or *someone,* should try to shed *some* brighter, more penetrating light on the underside of the Deconstruction that has cost society so much over the last twenty years or so in the way of literary waste and spoilage.

The case of Mariani versus Nason, I believe, is typical of thousands of identical contests between Deconstruction and its victims. I would prefer to use the example of somebody else's literary output other than my own as a case in point, but I must work with what I know — Mariani and Me, and I know no others so well. Now, would you for the sake of this kind of crucial experiment as to the nature of Deconstruction indulge me a little further and read one more excerpt from *A Modern Dunciad* (28 lines chosen at random — trust me! — pages 56–57), so we may proceed to the final steps of the experiment? Please do:

> Since verse by one could bear the other's name,
> And all were interchangeably the same,
> She *[Dullness — Pope's Device]* simply started with the letter "A"
> And asked the alphabet to lead the way.
> Then with a finger as a dousing-fork,
> She down the girded "A"'s just let it walk:
> From "Aiken," "Amis," "Ammons," it went on,
> Until it reached the name "Ashbery, John"!
> That name, however she might push or shove,
> Was like a magnet to the joint above,
> And wouldn't let her move it up or down,
> Until she pledged "Ashbery, John" the crown!
> How right she was to let the Fates prevail:
> A Harvard Grad who won a prize at Yale![1] *[numbers indicate footnotes]*
> Who felt that verse so badly failed the age
> Because it had not put the sound of Cage,[2]
> With all the force of calligraphs by Kline,[3]
> Enjoined with Beckett's analogic line,
> Into a kind of Audenesque address,
> That doubles back with Stevens-like finesse,[4]
> And by a subtle overlay of optics,[1]
> Is shattered as the shuttered gaze of Coptics,
> To give our age a dazzling sense of Self
> That might compete with Prufrock on the shelf!
> "Now this," he told O'Hara, "we should do,
> If for no other reason than it's new!
> Then once it's done, the future could be spent
> In asking people what we really meant!"

Got it? Good! Now — please! — take one more minute and return to the opening paragraph of Mariani's review quoted above: Read it carefully once again, and now tell me, honestly, placing the review side-by-side with the poem, and so with the evident character of the author, could you — or anyone — conceivably concoct the impression of the author that Mariani has presented to you, fully confident that he can make sure you most likely will have no chance to get any other impression of him?

On the basis of the poem itself, of which the brief quoted passage is a fair sample, would you — by any stretch of imagination or literary license — conclude that I was the kind of person, or "character" in the Aristotelian sense, who could be honestly depicted as the fey, furtive ineffectual figure he represents me to be — that I could be character-istically represented as one who "seems to keep shifting for the door, taking two cocktails with him while he mumbles something [there's that "something" again; Mariani is a master of the "something," rendering simple objections impossible — *that's* what I have meant when I referred to Deconstruction as sophistic!] under his breath about the goddam ill-bred decadence of all poetry since the death of the good Doctor Sam Johnson. . . ."

As you can now see for yourself, there is no evidence in the poem that I typically "shift" my ground. I've spent forty years gaining a firm height from which I project my satire in the *Dunciad.* I never descend from it out of subterfuge or shyness as Mariani's cartoon — unrelated to the actual features of its subject — would have you think. And, now, as you can discover for yourself, there are no "mumbles" in my poem, "under my breath," or over it. Read the excerpt from the *Dunciad* again if you must: You will find *no* "mumbles" — the exact opposite in fact. The language is consistently blunt and direct — most outspoken as to my strong feelings in the matters I discuss, in keeping with my *unshift-ing* purpose to satirize sharply. So much for the false impression Mariani works so cannily to convey as to the *tone* and *voice* of the poem and the nature of its author.

Now as to his contrived misrepresentation of the *substance* of the poem: He tells you I am satirizing "the goddam ill-bred decadence of all poetry since the death of the good Doctor Sam Johnson. . . ." My meaning throughout the poem (as a quotation in Chapter V, from the opening pages of the *Dunciad,* confirms) is the exact opposite. The thesis of my poem is the decline of poetry in the last *twenty-five years* as set against the antithesis, the contrast of Post-postmodern poetry to the poetry of the previous three hundred years. In order to set off the emptiness and banality and lack of distinction in our poetry today, I salute in literally hundreds of lines the inspiring role that poetry has played in Western culture back to antiquity up until about 1965 and the advent of what I call Neo-Existential poetry as exemplified by John Ashbery and hundreds of other poets just like him (including Mariani) writing *today,* who have only a wart or twitch to set them apart. I do not deplore these poets on the basis of their "ill-bred decadence" — the phrase itself is ridiculous, it means nothing — and is, by the way, a perfect example of Deconstructionist idiom in both form and substance, which we should note as part of our exercise in deconstructing Deconstruction. "Ill-bred decadence" — could there conceivably be any other kind, well-bred decadence, for instance? Should we not pause here to add a term to Deconstruction's "how to" books? If an oxymoron — one of its favorite "sightings," as in birdwatching — is a pointed contradiction in terms, could we not name such misnomers as "ill-bred decadence" multimorons, or a compacted redundancy?

But let me get right to it. My objection to the Neo-Existential poets, as laid out emphatically throughout the length of my *Duncaid,* is not that they are "ill-bred," but that they are "in-bred," that they are over-bred to the point of paralysis — that their style is *over*-cultivated to the point of archness, to the extent of a preciostic mannerliness, that they are, in fact, not Post-postmodern as they might present themselves, but archaic to the degree of social enervation and cultural exhaustion, that they are a throwback 250 years to the Baroque, or 100 years to the Georgian, that were the withering ends of more vigorous eras that came right before, that of Pope on the one hand, and of Tennyson on the other. So — as you may see if you are ever able to read the poem — I castigate Ashbery, and the hundreds of others who copy him or happen to coincide historically in the same literary fad or fashion, for being epicene, empty, vainglorious and vapid. And, last but not least, I find them cultural, social and literary cowards!

As to the "decadence," as in "goddam ill-bred decadence": Hell, the poets I deprecate in the *Dunciad* — Ashbery and his ilk — wouldn't *dare* to be decadent. It takes guts to be decadent. Like François Villon (Don't jump on him, Paul, he's just one of the hundreds of examples down through history — Hart Crane and Anne Sexton are more recent ones, as are dozens of others I praise in the *Dunciad,* who came after "the good Doctor Sam Johnson"). Ashbery is not decadent. It takes a sharp mind and a great imagination, like Baudelaire's, to be decadent. Ashbery might get a little testy sometimes, but "ill-bred"? Impossible! He'll accept "very clever," I'm sure. Or maybe make a concession to "snide." But we've already pointed out that oldster-Hippie flippancy, as in his case, does not constitute satire. And as to "ill-bred"? How could *I* ever make *that* the basis for my dismissal of others? Nobody could be more ill-bred than I am—I'm trying not to boast—unless it was the "good Doctor Sam Johnson" himself. And as to Paul Mariani's further false picture of me as "shifting for the door" while the drinks on the house seem to be still flowing—not on your life. The whole picture is a libel!

As to one or two more specifics in this case, Mariani exudes great gobs of feigned remorse at my "pathetic" failure as a poet, as if I might be afflicted with some mental deficiency or a crippling personality disorder that had deluded me into thinking I could jam an eighteenth-century sensibility into the twentieth century by simply putting on the clothes of the earlier period or merely adopting its poetic forms. He would have you think that *A Modern Dunciad* bears *no* relevance to our own immediate society and its widespread literary abuses, that it is so devoid of present reality, of *topicality,* that he *must*—despite his painful sympathies for me—warn you away from the awful embarrassment of turning the pages of my book. He writes:

> But there is something almost pathologically perverse about attacking Ashbery's poetry with early eighteenth-century smoothbores, and I find Nason's verbal assaults turning ineffectually against himself. . . .

And so on. A little later, Mariani states:

> . . . A Modern Dunciad . . . is a sad book, written by a man so stung by defeat, neglect and disappointment that he feels compelled to fire his loaded brace of pistols into the garish and crowded Op Art cocktail room where a number of New York's literary lights have gathered. What could sting a man so much that he would choose to reject the entire Romantic tradition to return to the so-called Age of Enlightenment, don the breeches and stocking hose of a Pope, and then quixotically attack the smart set in those terms?

Well, let me tell you further, Paul—but first let's allow our readers to see what we're talking *about*—the poem itself again. Mariani reserves special scorn for the way I have used Pope's devices to crown Ashbery the King of Dullness. Let's look at a couple of more excerpts—to see just how I presented that—and then proceed to decide which one of us is pulling whose what. Here, in this passage (page 58), John is in Paris (1955–65) when he's elected by the Goddess somewhere in New York (the book was half footnotes, which Mariani also scorns, to establish my claims for its historical accuracy and its biographical validity):

> So when the Goddess chose him at that hour
> He stood in shadow of Our Lady's *[Notre Dame's]* tower,[4]
> And couldn't see his own impending reign,
> But only sunset sinking in the Seine —
> For ever since he first arrived in France
> His shadow had been tutor to mischance:
> He heavily had shed Manhattan air,
> Because he said, the present wasn't there;
> Yet once in France, and travel as he might,
> The morning aged to noon, noon grew to night;
> And in what often seemed the final wrench,
> He found that all of France spoke only French;[5]
> While in the States, the critics through misprise,
> Reduced to kindling-wood his sapling "Trees!"[6] *[His first book]*

The many footnotes lend detailed timely context to the allusions. And, as I say, it was a "true" description of Ashbery during his ten years in Paris, where, he later actually stated, he would have preferred to paint, but his room there was not big enough for the canvasses and easel, so he decided to write poetry instead. My poem, I say again, captures the *ennui* and affectation — and the awful pettiness — that John Ashbery later in fact presented to the world through his poetry. For instance, Ashbery's favorite image was to become the mirror — I suggest how he got used to mirrors, his own reflection, that is, in Paris (page 60):

> When all at once, while looking in the glass,
> The mirror summoned him: "Attend, you ass![1]
> Too much self-scrutiny," it slowly spoke,
> "Is still bad luck, you know!" And then it broke!
> The glass, in splintered sections, with its sheen,
> Fell with the keenness of a guillotine,
> And severed, with a crunch upon the floor,
> The imaged head that it had held before;
> As surely as a blade against the neck
> It slew that poet in the crystal wreck!

Does Mariani *really* find this poetry so poor as to signify nothing more than the "perversity" and "pathology" of its author? Or is it not — in our time of cloying Post-postmodern unanimity — fresh and new in the central points it would make, and somewhat amusing in the way that it makes them? What do *you* think of it? Or this, when the Goddess Dullness flounces to Paris to put Ashbery back together and subdue the fire he has set to his as-yet-unaccepted poetry (page 75):

> Which to undo, great Dullness was aroused
> To save the Laureate she had just espoused:
> She hopped upon her trusty mattress warmer,
> Whose shape and size inspired the Backfire Bomber,
> And as the winds our longitudes elide,
> She heaved herself to Paris and his side!
> Her presence in his room soon stifled all,
> John's siege of sense and the ensuing pall:
> She wiggled once and wooed him with his name;
> The mirror was restored; so sank the flame!
> The poet wakened as the mortal slept;
> Then down the Paris skies the Goddess swept
> By laser beam with only brief ado
> From Paris to New York, where John came to
> Within her bunker and her mighty arms,
> To cheers and tributes and police alarms!
> The Goddess had, you see, to Koch confided,
> A son of Cibber would be soon provided:
> Then Koch told Kornblee, Kornblee, Cott,[1]
> Cott, Kostelanetz, who just told the lot!
> The wily Goddess knew no public line
> Spread secrets faster than her college vine.
> And so upon that fabled day of days
> Ashbery, John sat up to sudden praise,
> And found his suite could boast of more display
> Than all the auction rooms at Parke-Bernet!
> Motif of Crême, cerise and citrus shade:
> "O, this will match my poem on lemonade!" *[a footnote quotes this poem]*
> He cried, obliquely lest we all forget
> He turns "hello" into a whole "Quartet"! *[And the poem that makes this point]*

As difficult as it might be to savor all this without the sauces and garnishes of the footnotes, which further concretize the preposterous pretensions of our Post-postmodern poets and pundits, I think you might by now agree that the muzzle-velocity of my satire somewhat exceeds that of the "smoothbore" or antique "brace of pistols" Mariani invokes to characterize my diction, when he writes:

> . . . But by choosing as his weapon something as outmoded in this country as the Heroick Couplet . . . Nason is savaging himself, actively courting defeat, as if he meant to go out in a fiery but meaningless blaze of glory. And for me the touchstone of Nason's failure rests in the pathetic way in which he quotes Ashbery [which Mariani

says makes Ashbery seem better than ever].... Clearly the literary
polis of late twentieth-century New York is not early eighteenth-
century London. The very terms of the debate lie on either side of the
Great Divide created by Rousseau and Blake, Wordsworth and
Goethe....

We must pause here for a moment in this, our early exercise in
deconstructing Deconstruction. As in all such collegiate sophistry,
Mariani must put in place of the sense of my poem something that
dismisses itself as a patent falsehood. Of course, I know that our present literary *polis* is not that of the past, as I have made unmistakably
clear throughout the entire *Modern Dunciad* and in my current efforts
to describe further Post-postmodernism in the present book.

But we must say a few more words about Paul Mariani's reference
to the "Great Divide created by Rousseau and Blake, Wordsworth and
Goethe." Do you, fond reader, my confederate in all this, know what
he's talking about? Well, I do. Such references as that to the "Great
Divide" have themselves become clichés during the several decades of
Deconstruction. Their employment as reflexive maneuvers in Deconstructionist polemics has become as standard as the milk separator in
dairy-farming, to free the curdling, disposable premodern from the
presumed cream of the postmodern, to persuade us that poetry assumed its patent modernity sometime in the early 1800s with the introduction of poetic reflections on the way poetry is written and the
manner in which it performs, within the poem itself. What this states
is that the Later Romantic extended Early Romantic sensibility to include an ongoing expression of the way the poet's mind worked as a
bridge between its own functions and all perceived objects and structured relations in the "real" world.

Mariani would have you think that this contest between competing
aesthetic systems, or epistemologies, is closed; and that Ashbery and
he are secure on the firmer, preferred modern side of the "Great
Divide"; and that any poetry imputing fixed entities in the "real" or objective world has missed the last bus to outer space. This is utter
nonsense, as we will begin to see when we further assess such distinctions in pages to come of the present exercise in deconstructing
Deconstruction. But if we are to defend ourselves right now against
the corrosive acids of Neo-Existential critiques like Mariani's, based
upon oldish notions like that of the "Great Divide," we must invoke
the powerful but still mostly unremarked undercurrents already at
work beneath Deconstruction. They have already made the critical

ground he's standing on precarious indeed. And soon a tide arising just ahead may carry him out of the mainstream, where he still thinks he is, far, far beyond the point of no return.

His "Great Divide," in fact, has turned out to be an alienating gulf of impassable distances and dangerous disproportions. It is true that it *critically* supports an ever wider tolerance for what some call today a new Formalism, that is, for the *act* of writing as the *subject* of the writing. And indeed, Wordsworth may have been a liberating advance on Rousseau. But Mariani — and his Neo-Existential tribe in academia — should be warned that the narrower and narrower focus of recent poetry and criticism upon its own processes, as far back as Auden, began to present itself, not as simply a daring philosophical exploration with no closure in sight — as Mariani obviously still supposes it to be — but as an arbitrary and meaningless dead-end where poetry itself must disappear altogether. For if Wordsworth and Goethe (along with hundreds of other noted poets since them) ventured most carefully and tentatively along these metaphysical departures from the past, they never dared forget the overwhelming substantiality of the world around them. To do so is to court ultimate absolute peril in our own history, as we today continue to do, as I've been at considerable pains and other expense to say loudly and clearly in the pages of *A Modern Dunciad.*

It may be that Late Romantic and even postmodern poetry attempted to invigorate both the objective world and the presence of the poet in it by expressing strategies of composition and processes of perception, by making *them* a part of the poem, by giving *them* within the poem the same significance as substantial objects and categorical relations from the "real" world. And by so doing, through the primal, reciprocal exchanges within such subjective–objective dichotomies, somehow strengthened and augmented our human presence in the great scheme of the cosmos. It struggled this way to confer on poetry, on the poem itself, the authority and durability of a natural manifestation — of a rock, a river, or a tree perhaps — insisting the poem becomes "part of imperishable nature," even as it remains part of perishable humankind, like Stevens' now-notorious "jar in Tennessee." But the final effect of this interchangeability of real object and poetic construct in the poetry of Ashbery (and you, Paul) has been to act to dissolve the cosmos altogether and thereby obliterate its own aesthetic basis.

And that's where we are today. On the edge of a metaphysical collapse. And this breakdown has as its literary equivalent the poetry I condemn — and for these same reasons — in *A Modern Dunciad*. Paul Mariani better crawl out of the "Great Divide" long enough to look around and realize that while such Deconstructionist buzz phrases may still play well in Peoria and Amherst, many books are now being written that will make Paul and his pals more outdated than my Heroick Couplets.

Post-postmodernists like Mariani throw around such shibboleths and rubrics as "the Great Divide" to give their polemics an intimidating aspect. For example, Deconstruction — and especially Neo-Existential poetry — has carried over from modern science — from Einstein's Relativity, for instance — the false beliefs that the objective, perceived world has no fixed forms and, more crucially, that mankind has no predisposition to ethical norms — that, in sum, what you see as "real" and what you feel as "good" are both relative. Einstein himself was most insistent in his repeated warnings (beginning with his Special Theory of Relativity in 1905) that mankind should not make the mistake of generalizing *his* findings, from the mathematical actions of matter, to the behavioral actions of human beings. In other words, that the human nervous system — our way of seeing, feeling, and behaving — should not be logically subjected to his revisions of Newtonian physics. In fact, he regarded such a possibility as a potential disaster on a par with the impending threat of nuclear weapons.

Yet Post-postmodern literature seems grossly unaware or positively indifferent to such serious warnings. It goes much further in this respect than even Einstein could have predicted. This recent poetry — and its commentary, denser than a blizzard of trash at a ticker-tape parade — has not only ruptured normal sensory processes, describing matter as a kind of silly putty, but has also short-circuited innate human ethical categories, presenting faith and morality as a kind of schized-up Punk Rock light show. Herein lies the vaunted "novelty" and the contrived "mystery" of Post-postmodern literature. It is based mainly on what I might now label "the scientistic fallacy," which should eventually take its place beside "the pathetic fallacy" as a poetic taboo. For if it is mistaken to claim that nature has human faculties (the essence of the pathetic fallacy, Paul) it is equally mistaken to say that human beings exhibit the mathematical characteristics of cosmic nature as set forth by Einstein.

But we should expect that a master of the "Great Divide" like Paul Mariani would be equally adept at the scientistic fallacy in his fallaciously inferred relativity of language. Wouldn't you know that the main basis for his high estimation of Ashbery's poetry is to be found in modern science. I anticipated this spurious argument from modern science to support Post-postmodernism's metaphysick (there now, Paul, I hand you back that crappy extra "k" you put in my Heroick Couplet) at considerable length in *A Modern Dunciad*. Good god — we've been reading this foolish gobbledygook about relative human perception and relative human behavior in mass-consumer magazines like *The Reader's Digest* since the end of the Second World War. It was inevitable that Pop poets like Ashbery would bring it over as the distinguishing stamp of Neo-Existential poetry. And that people like Mariani would subscribe to it now as part of the Neo-Existential world view. In the last twenty years Einstein has been joined by Heisenberg with his Uncertainty Principle as an unwitting tool of Post-postmodern aestheticians. They shanghai many others onto their ship. But Mariani mentions Einstein and Heisenberg specifically in his leap over my *Dunciad* into the "Great Divide":

> . . . [W]e cannot employ the diction and parallel syntax and terminal rhymes of Pope convincingly in our time any more than we can give imaginative assent to the absolutism of a Newtonian Universe to explain our world today. We may not like such a state of affairs any more perhaps than Harold Bloom and John Ashbery or others like it [don't let Mariani kid you — they all love it — and the monthly windfall of checks it brings], but it appears to be our particular terrain of hell in which we find ourselves; at least these men have tapped into the random and radically asymmetrical patterns of thought which — since Einstein and Heisenberg — appear to be our age's particular (and peculiar) signature.

That "peculiar" is prophetic. Thirteen years ago, I *knew* someone just like Paul Mariani would be saying exactly *that* about my mock-epic poem. I anticipated as many of his twists and turns as I could, which we must do if we would undertake our deconstruction of Deconstruction. Pages 15–16 of *Dunciad:*

> Let's take this modern poet's wide ellipse
> And pull it in a knot that never slips
> And lead him through the streets of Cambridge, Mass.,
> For throwing stones at Shelley's dome of glass:
> We'll let his students get a look at him
> And then we'll throw his empty book at him!
> We'll chain him to the arch in Greenwich Village
> To put an end to Eliotic pillage,

The wanton plunder of de Kooning's palette,
The verse effect of Op with melting wallet;
At Bard, we'll book him as a hideous felon
For drinking on his grant from Andrew Mellon;
At Berkeley, charge him thus: syntax offender,
Excess reflective verbs, the neuter gender.
So many marvels will we soon retrieve
From cuffs that out-finesse a Chinese sleeve,
We'll find the pea beneath the walnut dome:
The trick is in the poet, not the poem.

Those pedants *[Mariani]* who declare the age is dead
That ever needed Pope or Dunciad,
His couplet now, too narrow for our space,
His measure, Newton's feet in Einstein's race,
Have been undone by Dullness' utter ruse,
Whereby she argues sense outlives its use,
And that the Universe, by math so curved,
Entails us to deny the thing observed.
Since space and time, she soars, are relative,
And clocks regress with speed and rulers give,
We must expand this mathematic metaphor
To slow and shrink the mind so less is more.
Thus Dullness drapes the poet's *[Ashbery's]* lupine lies
In sheepskins of a scientific guise,
And deems those bards most surely up-to-date
Who can with crypto-science obfuscate,
Compose their poems from cold, remote relations,
Consigning mundane things to spatial stations,
Omit the mortal theme that won't be right
Unless divided by the speed of light;
Who, since a moral might arise in rhyme,
Write only poems that chirr and ping and chime,
Who hold that Fate won't damn us or exhort us
Because of all that science now has taught us;
That fire can't wither, ice won't scathe, that sex
Has no connection with an age complex,
That pity is passé and passion rank
In light of Fermi, Bohr and Max Karl Planck.
Hence Dullness, in the Summa of her error:
O, Ecce Homo, in a convex mirror![1]
        [Ashbery's Pulitzer poem was "Self-Portrait in a Convex Mirror"]

As we see, despite what Mariani might say about it, my *Modern Dunciad* provides a pretty good blueprint of the Post-postmodernist establishment — and might serve as a nifty guide as to just how we might go about deconstructing it. We still must take the final steps in this undertaking. For one thing, sooner or later we will have to ascertain to what extent proponents of Deconstructionist criticism and Neo-Existential poetry reject, suppress or censor other aesthetic systems that might challenge their hegemony within the university system, the poetry publishing business and along the lecture circuit. The collusion is vast and has so many tenuous points of interconnectedness that it is most difficult to pin it down, as we find in the case of my own *Dunciad*.

Richard Walton, a veteran political journalist and historian, insists that my book was "censored" by the Neo-Existential poetry network in a way that could only be described as a concerted violation of the spirit of the Bill of Rights through "a conspiracy of silence." Paul Mariani scoffs at such a prospect as being beyond the realm of possibility. But is it really?

Perhaps you, dear reader, can help us decide. For, in truth, although a stinking rat may not be a smoking gun, the integrity and credibility of literature today hang upon the disposition of several ulterior questions like this. So I would like to invite anyone reading this who has evidence of these kinds of practices within our current literary establishment to submit his or her firsthand evidence to The Smith, or to McFarland.

One more thing: Mariani, while talking about Walton's profile of me in the *Village Voice* cited earlier, slyly inserts as fact that "*A Modern Dunciad* has met with a deafening silence on all fronts." This, too, is false. In Chapter VII, we'll see what actually happened. And this won't be a matter of opinion, or a case of Mariani's "misreading" versus Nason's "misreading," but a flint-sharp point of fact. My *Dunciad* was warmly welcomed wherever it appeared beyond the choking overgrowth of the Neo-Existential critical network. It sold thousands of copies, mainly by word of mouth. Walton concluded his informal canvass of national reaction by writing, "Despite establishment silence . . . *[A Modern Dunciad]* . . . has become something of an underground classic. . . ." Well, I don't like this "underground classic" stuff much either — that's another collegiate stereotype, and is not the point I want to make here, which is, that Mariani typifies the Post-postmodernist establishment in the way he attempts to block our view of what else in the way of poetry and criticism might be available out there!

Meanwhile, one more parting shot from my "pathetic" "smoothbore": Mariani's "Great Divide" actually refers back to something much deeper, much more distant and much more difficult to describe than the cleavage between Rousseau and Blake and Goethe and

Wordsworth he mentions. Though it cannot be batted around so
buoyantly by "the literary lights" in "the smart set" — *his* crowd — it is
much closer to the facts, to state that the literary chasm was created
by the historical forces of an earlier time, as Eliot insisted finally such
cleavages are (see Chapter III). Specifically, the gulf between Blake
and Wordsworth was caused by a profound parallel fault within metaphysics a hundred years earlier between John Locke and George
Berkeley on the far side and Baron von Leibniz and Immanuel Kant
on the more modern side, all of whom were establishing their theories
around the age of Pope.

I doubt that Mariani and Ashbery are able to sort out what really
is happening in our own literary era. But an inquiry into this much
greater "Great Divide" reveals that Ashbery conforms to the older out-
moded position of Locke and Berkeley. With them, Ashbery obviously believes there are no fixed or innate qualities — such as dimension and color — in objective reality — and no such thing as human nature — such as a predisposition to fixed ethical systems. I'm sure it
would surprise both Mariani and Ashbery to realize that the same outdated metaphysical world they share with Locke and Berkeley was
also shared by Alexander Pope. I, on the other hand, more than forty
years ago, advanced with the rest of the world to the conclusions of
Kant, synthesizing Leibniz's rationalism with Locke's empiricism,
Berkeley's idealism and Hume's skepticism, reasserting the primacy of
a tough fixed physical universe and a hard biologically structured
system of human ethics, which Kant's predecessors — including
Pope — tended to question.

May I ask you, Paul, do you and Ashbery know you are both in the
same metaphysical bed with the despised Pope, not with Goethe and
Wordsworth at all? And that I, strangely and contrariwise, adhering
to the more recent and hence more modern synthesis of Kant, demonstrate a philosophical outlook in my verse that owes more to Wordsworth (Keats is a richer reference in my case) and Goethe than to
either Pope, Ashbery or Mariani?

More urgently, Paul, you should warn Ashbery that he dooms his
poetry to an early death by plugging into Einstein and Heisenberg,
as they themselves could have told him. Tell him also that your shared
scientistic fallacy lies along the still greater "Great Divide" between
perception and *apperception*.

The breach in Neo-Existential aesthetics is wider than the Milky
Way itself. Fifty years from now, Ashbery will be only three sentences

in a lengthy footnote. And Paul Mariani will not be mentioned at all.

This final volley from my Colonial pistols should serve as a warning to all aspiring Deconstructionist critics and Neo-Existential poets plunging after the shabby trophies of Post-postmodernism, that they must look before they leap. Otherwise, like Mariani, they might find themselves in a much deeper "Great Divide" than they bargained for.

Chapter VII. Deconstruction Finally Takes Us to the End of the Line.

We must now hop off to join the growing forces of Reconstruction to restore poetry and criticism to their former place of authority in American culture.

It has taken more than 20 years for Deconstruction to get rid of common sense. It will be no easy job to restore it. Undertaking all this is like digging a ditch from Sheridan Square to Lincoln Center with a teaspoon. I would frankly rather be doing something else. This whole business with Bloom and Ashbery has made me dizzy. Thank god the end is just ahead. Meanwhile, to resume, let's face it: deconstructing Deconstruction raises more questions than we can sensibly clutch, comprehend and convey, like bread thrown in the midst of feeding pigeons. We need a new kind of wide-angle buckshot, when, as Paul Mariani has so kindly pointed out, I have nothing but a "smoothbore" — the English Language.

First, why have I used my own *A Modern Dunciad* in this public exercise? Isn't that in bad taste? Yes, probably. But I had no choice. No one else had the same experience or the same opportunity to do it. I can only remind you there are important precedents for such strategies. For instance, Pope himself used to write pseudonymous negative reviews of his own poems. Then, using his own name, he would excoriate the traducers. It worked beautifully. I find this blunt approach somehow more appealing than the standard practice within the Neo-Existential establishment today where virtually every poem or critique that appears in its name turns out to be either immediately or remotely the result of some sort of connivance.

Next, what do I mean by Neo-Existential? Not very much. Twenty-five years ago these little poems that dwell on nothing but themselves seemed curiosities—strange new shells on the beach. Remember Newton? When they asked him what it was like hooking up the connections in his gravitational system, he is said to have answered, "like gathering shells at the seashore." Or something along that line. Now from that sublime to this ridiculous, when I first began to see all these weird little poems littering the beach I wondered where I was when the storm churned them up from the bottom. I'd pick them up one at a time and turn them between my fingers. What in hell's name were they? I didn't really know. But they reminded me of something. I remembered—the definitions of Existentialism I had read in high school or college—experiences disconnected from both memory and prediction with no conceivable reach or resonance beyond themselves. That's what I mean by Existential. And as to the Neo, I simply say we've seen it all before.

In sum, what is Deconstruction? It is an effort to reverse the ratio of writer to reader. To make the reader larger than the writer. I could say I find this disturbing. That would be like whispering at the top of a hurricane, "It's very windy." In fact, I find it insane, like having God sit at the feet of man. It deranges nature without adding anything in the way of humor, loveliness or enlightenment. Where did Deconstruction come from? When? Yale University. Circa 1965. Then it spread westward like an unidentified plague. Geoffrey Hartman, a carrier of Teutonic metaphysics, sneezed first. In the line of spray were Harold Bloom and the late Paul de Man. But the retrovirus mutated in them, prompting an end run (to enrich the metaphorical mixture for more speed) around Hartman's Germanic game plan to pick up laterals from France's Jacques Derrida and his team. There are hundreds of books on all this stuff. Keep away from them if you have not been inoculated against academic circumlocutions. They will render you unfit for any kind of direct response to your immediate surroundings. Know just enough about these characters to identify them in the name of strict avoidance. Just enough to sympathize with their affliction, but never so much that you envy their advance beyond you to tenure and higher pay by virtue of their as-if-steroid-boosted strength in hurling around huge boxcar-sized terms like Deconstruction and Post-structuralism.

What is the relation of Deconstruction in criticism to Neo-Existentialism in poetry? Too close for comfort. In fact, I lump them together. I use them interchangeably. Not because Bloom has finally persuaded me as to the equivalency of poetry and prose. You'd be crazier than he is if you believed that. But because both Deconstruction and Neo-Existential poetry became melted together in the same Post-postmodern time warp: again, New Haven, Connecticut, around 1965. That's when Bloom came out of the closet of traditional criticism on the lookout for an Ashbery or two. And that's when Ashbery came back from Paris. John, you may remember, had won a Yale Younger Poet Award a decade earlier. Ashbery reappeared none too soon. Bloom needed him desperately. What the hell — he was in the process of reducing all great poetry from Homer to T. S. Eliot to so much odoriferous, disposable prose. He had to have some contemporaries to maintain the whole business as an ongoing enterprise. Bloom's purpose was to prove that poetry is meaningless. That is, that it means *everything*. And that, therefore, everything (a popsicle stick, an old shoe, an exclamation of "wow!"), anything at all is a poem. Since this is one's point, why shouldn't one single out as the "best modern poets" people like Ashbery and Ammons who have demonstrated over many, many years no penetrating gift for writing it in the first place. It worked out well for all of them.

This ever-so-brief primer of terms prepares us to advance to the final steps in our exercise: deconstructing Deconstruction. Is there a network of poets out there with a collective purpose of promoting a Neo-Existential mystique as both a way of writing and a way of life? Certainly there is. And does this network undertake as its first priority the exclusion of outsiders to preserve teaching posts, publications, highly paid appearances on panels and reading tours for themselves? Absolutely. Does this then call for censorship of much literature to maintain the "integrity" of the network? Yes, at every turn. Squeeze it off at the point of publication if you can. If it slips through, get rid of it by "a conspiracy of silence." How can you prove there is a network and that it suppresses competing material? You can't. A sharp focus is needed to establish anything by proof. The world of Neo-Existential poetry has as its central device the fuzzing of all focus on everything, most assuredly on any attack upon itself. Then what should we do? Wait for the tide that dropped all this crap on the beach to carry it back out to sea. And read on.

Network? Censorship? How could these things exist when one of the enforcing tenets of the Neo-Existential establishment today is that real human beings are really not involved in the enterprise at all? After its work on all literary fronts over more than two decades you're

supposed to know that all this cosmical junk poetry and criticism just
sort of floats our way out of nowhere. That's simply the way literary
history is presented in the nevernever land of academia. Things just
happen. Either you get it or you don't. If you start thinking of flesh-
and-blood matters such as personal motivation and private intentions,
you'll get pinned with the scarlet B for blasphemy.

That's why Paul Mariani could adopt such a sacerdotal tone in dis-
missing my *Modern Dunciad*. He looked upon my description of all his
deconstructed poet-friends as clowns and freaks as a dangerous
heresy. That's why he had to stigmatize its author as a pariah. Contact
with my books would invite literary excommunication. He draped me
with the adjectival sackcloths of "pathetic" and "pathologically
perverse." "What could sting a man so much," he inquires pontifically
in the *Parnassus* review, ". . . that he would quixotically attack the
smart set . . . and feels compelled to fire his loaded brace of pistols into
the garish and crowded Op Art cocktail room where a number of New
York's literary lights have gathered. . . ." In other words, what are *you*
doing here?

These poets and commentators regard themselves as the quasi-
spiritual fathers of our society. In the manner of the Georgian poets,
they look upon themselves as otherworldly. Many, many years ago,
Richard Howard wrote a long, long poem for *The New Yorker* describing poets today as "monks" preserving our cultural treasures from bar-
barian depredations in their gold-crusted scrolls. This sandaled stance
serves to isolate the new poets from the critical intrusions of the world
beyond their monastic order. The very idea of inquiring after their
methods, manners or morals!

This sanctimonious psychic thrust originates in the poems themselves. They are presented as sublime, impersonal artifacts. I attempted to deal with this weird quality in my preface to *Old Soldiers*
(1989):

> . . . I know there is a long-standing prohibition against appending
> a prose statement like this to a poem. If you look to the reasons, you
> will find they stem mainly from a kind of superstition. The poet who
> says *anything* at all about his poem runs the risk of demystifying it and
> thereby reducing its aura as a magical object. This aversion is part-
> and-parcel of the more general attempt to make a poem a quasi-
> religious artifact, ineffable in its effects and divine in its origins. A
> Preface may cancel these residual effects in that it suggests the poem
> is sensible in its fabrication of something merely human, therefore
> both mortal in its nature and personal in its source. . .

Poems written within this Neo-Existential mystique work to reduce
the world to a figment of the poet's imagination. They also serve to
desubstantiate the poets themselves. These characters come at you as
emissaries from a collective dream. They are most apt to present
themselves as magicians who can render the deadly horrors of this
world deceptively harmless by turning them into examples of modern
art. They see the whole world as a kind of elegant Uptown *salon* full
of potentially profitable Pop or Op Art. Charles Simic, our latest
Pulitzer, exemplifies this as if by complicit ordination. Show him
anything at all and he'll turn it into a word-powered modern painting.
Simic is almost a science-fiction clone of the early John Ashbery. John
was the leading composer of prose poems in his day. He's tired of it
lately. But Charles picks up right where John left off. Like John, he
also tries to plug into the economic and social authority of modern art.
On the occasion of his award, Simic walked about the City dispensing
Neo-Existential profundities in the company of reporter Mervyn
Rothstein, who described this historic stroll in *The New York Times*
(November 9, 1990):

> ". . . The city is like a piece of modern art" [the reporter quotes the
> poet]. "You should just delight in the act of looking, without trying
> immediately to reach a conclusion about what you are seeing. In so
> many modern poems, we don't have any conclusions or morals or
> messages. It is not a question of what does it all mean. With this city,
> you cannot ask that question."

The reporter catches the Neo-Existential virus:

> . . . Look at a crowd of people for example. Just another crowd?
> Not to Mr. Simic. Sometimes it's like a peaceful scene from Bruegel.
> But it depends on the crowd. If there's a lot of pushing and shoving,
> it's more like a canvas by Bosch, with its sea of humanity, tortured and
> damned for eternity . . . [hot stuff!].

Simic penetrates to the very bedrock of his philosophy, as quoted by
the reporter:

> He points in the air. "There," he says. "And there. And there [pointing
> toward the water towers]. The first thing you think of when you look
> at them is that they're ugly. But then after a while you look again and
> they're beautiful. They're like a symbol of the city. One thing I like
> about New York is that it's ugly. There's a wonderful anarchy. New
> York has all the ugliness and terror of the 20th century. But if you look
> closely, all the beauty and sublimity is there, too."
> On a street down near SoHo, Mr. Simic finds another little detail:

on the side of a grocery store there is a painting, appropriately enough of a stand of grocery shelves, with cans and boxes and cereal cartons in vivid color.

"The city is a little like this painting," he says. "A lot of little items, come upon serendipitously. Or more precisely, there's an element of collage in this city. It's like the so-called primitive artists, who paint anything they like on their canvases, even if it doesn't fit together. If they like lions, they put in a little lion. If they like woods, they put that in too. You don't know why those things should be there, but if you keep them someday you'll find their secret relation. It's like the pieces of my poems...."

Just outside the park [Washington Square], Mr. Simic stops and looks at the sidewalk. On the ground, randomly scattered, are five abandoned shoes: two black boots, a blue sneaker and a pair of red pumps. To most people, the poet says, they are nothing but garbage. But to him, there is a composition, a haphazard design, an unintentional color scheme. There is for him, in this wretched refuse of our teeming shore, an art, a beauty, symbolic of New York.

And you ask where poetry's moral authority has gone? This guy's been talking to his freshmen at the University of New Hampshire too long. There are hundreds of Simics out there in our universities. The real world never hears about them until they win a Pulitzer, or better yet, get a MacArthur grant. They'd all win at least a Pulitzer if they lived long enough, except perhaps Allen Ginsberg. For all his expertise in leveraging largesse for himself and his Buddhist ashram, the slick Ashbery poets have for almost twenty years beaten Ginsberg out of his Pulitzer—Ashbery, Richard Howard, Donald Justice, a dozen others, and now Charles Simic. Poetry's a tough racket!

How are all these Simics incubated and presented to the world annually, not as pullets, but as Pulitzers? This question flies right back to our key exhibit in this case, my own *Dunciad*. Could it be an important example of just how the Neo-Existential establishment works to maintain its own hegemony? Was the *Dunciad* suppressed in New York City? And if so, how? And could it not represent literally thousands of similar cases over the last twenty years? *Some* answer to such a question is central to the whole process of deconstructing Deconstruction. Paul Mariani scoffs at such notions as "pathologically perverse." The Simics of this world would no doubt agree. These new poet-critic-professors present themselves as mystical entities devoid of merely human impulses. If in this sense they are not *real,* the rationalization runs, how could they collect in a network? And if there is no network, how could there be such a thing as censorship, either by "silence" or any other means?

Richard Walton is a troubleshooting political reporter. Book editor Eliot Fremont-Smith, apparently, having failed in his initial mission to get the *Dunciad* reviewed in *The Village Voice,* assigned Walton to do the story on me as the next best thing. Walton told me during the interview that he found all poetry uninteresting. He regarded my book mainly as an example of possible press censorship. And he had finally concluded it represented a patent case of "censorship by silence." I thought Walton would surely contact Fremont-Smith to find out what actually happened. To which reviewers did he give my book? And did they state any reason for not reviewing it? Walton regarded the instance as so obvious and blatant that he felt no need for further testimony in its proof. The first sentence in his piece simply stated it as fact: "This is about an extraordinary book that refuses to die, despite what seems to be a continuing conspiracy of silence in this city."

Unfortunately, Walton let it go at that—and so left the door open for Paul Mariani a year or so later to tell the whole world through the pages of *Parnassus* that this silly idea of "censorship by silence" was cooked up by Walton and me to type a book that was rejected for review in New York solely on the basis of its poor quality as poetry. One person who knows otherwise is Eliot Fremont-Smith. I suppose he's still around. Paul, perhaps you could ask him the next time you bump into him in one of those "garish and crowded Op Art cocktail rooms where a number of New York's literary lights have gathered." I'm sure he could help you get to the bottom of questions like this.

Well, Paul, no doubt, has been much too busy to bother with my trifling "sour grapes." He has probably been pasting up reviews of his recently published *Collected Poems* (November, 1990), mentally incorporating favorable reviewers into the network and getting rid of those opposed. Even so, our exercise demands that we deal with Paul's assertion in *Parnassus* that *A Modern Dunciad* "met with a deafening silence on all fronts." Here is a glaring and so a noteworthy example of how far these guys will go to make sure the public catches no glimpse of poetry other than their own. The facts are these, Paul: my book was fairly and enthusiastically reviewed in dozens of places beyond the reach of the Neo-Existential network both in this country and in cities as far-flung as Florence and Amsterdam.

In fact, may it haunt you forever that *A Modern Dunciad* has worked its way around the Neo-Existential blackball in New York mostly by word-of-mouth to where it has become a sort of rallying point against the day when poetry will be restored to a place of authority in our society. Eventually this counter literary movement will wrench the Bloom-Ashbery locks from university English department doors. But please walk away, Paul, with these words from the real world ringing in your ears — as chronicled in a foot-thick folder in my tipsy file cabinet:

From John McKernan, director of writing, Marshall University, Huntington, West Virginia, February 19, 1982:

> A letter to praise you for your brilliant *A Modern Dunciad*. I loved it. I screamed with laughter. It is so often so perfectly on target that I could scarcely believe anyone in our Braille-Bound Age could have composed it. Pope and Johnson would have loved it. I consider it the finest imitation of Pope's manner and style I have ever encountered. I am sending a copy to my former teacher Patricia Craddock — the Biographer of Gibbon who knows more of the 18th Century than any human alive — and I am convinced she will agree with me. . . . The entire book is witty, lively, intelligent and quick moving. My only suggestion is to write more. . . . I salute you and wish you well.

From Tom Clark, former editor of *The Paris Review,* in a review published in *The Denver Post,* April 20, 1980:

> Richard Nason's splendidly produced (and relatively inexpensive) "A Modern Dunciad" is justly proclaimed by its publisher as a current-day classic. It's a biting and funny verse attack on the present arts establishment in this country, done in the form and idiom of Alexander Pope's great, savage mock-epic of the 18th century. . . .
> . . . Nason revives Pope's basic concept — and his heroic couplet — with an adroitness that doubtless would have pleased the Twickenham poet himself.
> . . . Nason . . . sees a new dullness as having invaded the arts of this country — and in particular, the art of poetry. His is certainly a plausible proposition. In American poetry these days, reputations, grants, publications and positions sometimes appear to be apportioned according to a maddening principle of social cronyism that is very hard to identify with any literary value. It's to be expected that those comparatively disenfranchised authors who toil in obscurity would have complaints. Usually such complaints are voiced in desperate and private terms. Nason, however, here manages something much more publicly edifying (and funny) than a mere gripe.
> . . . To the position of modern-day laureate of Dullness, Nason appoints John Ashbery, author of very difficult poems in a mode particularly odious to Nason, which he terms "existential poetry." In

charting (with verse and copious footnotes) the graph of Ashbery's career, Nason presents an amusing template of the recent downfall of good sense in both American poetry and American culture in general. . . .

Clark's review concludes that the book is "crisply narrated in some of the finest comic verse anyone's produced in years." In a letter to Harry Smith, publisher of *A Modern Dunciad,* Tom Clark wrote further:

> . . . I found Nason's effort . . . quite inspiring in concept. Is he considering further such attempts? (If so, more power to him.) Ed Dorn [author of the noted *Gunslinger* and *Hello, La Jolla,* critic and teacher] was also impressed with Nason's book and may well intend to teach it in the future.

From Ed Dorn in Boulder, Colorado, to Harry Smith, May 22, 1980:

> Enclosed find payment for a copy of *Modern Dunciad* which I'd like you to send to Donald Davie [British poet then teaching in Nashville].
> I'm doing a job in Juneau, the month of June, and I'd like some copies of *Modern Dunciad* sent up there. The trouble is, I haven't sorted out where. I'll get in touch when I do and hope for the best.

From Donald Wesling, professor of English at the University of California, San Diego, undated:

> Edward Dorn (whom you may know) has advised that I purchase a "strange and stunning" book by Richard Nason, titled *A Modern Dunciad.* If you trust me enough to send the book to me with an invoice for price and postage, I'll send a check by return airmail. If you care instead to send a note telling the amount required, I'll be glad to send the check in advance.

From Warren Hope, poet and publisher of *Drastic Measures,* a semi-annual poetry quarto, Haverton, Pennsylvania, December 20, 1979, to Harry Smith:

> . . . I wanted to let you know that I heartily concur with your judgment of *A Modern Dunciad.* Had me laughing aloud on the train ride home. I think it compares favorably with the original not only because of the natural handling of the couplets but also because Richard Nason has more humor than Pope, lacks the latter's meanness of spirit (some of Pope's Dunces were men he paid poorly to do the literal translations of Homer Pope versified, etc.), and sticks to the work much more than personalities. Book the Fourth is a wonderful romp. Especially liked the bits on Harold Bloom's "criticism". . . .

From Stephen Philbrick, Massachusetts sheep raiser and poet, in a review in *The Providence Journal,* April 9, 1979:

> Surprise yourself. Buy this book. After all, it's probably the only book-length essay on contemporary poetry that you'll buy this year, and certainly the only one written in rhymed couplets....
>
> ... Ideally, Ashbery and his baited brethren would respond with an angry pamphlet or a nasty blast. Such plainspoken bravery seems a bit public and gauche for them, however. They'll probably try to ignore Nason and The Smith publicly, while vowing to blackball them from the sorts of fellowships and committees that they'd never apply for anyway. Such sloth is the best weapon of the literary establishment. Dullness cloaks her own.
>
> I admire Nason. In the literary jungle, where no back is left unstabbed, he has had the courage to wage a full frontal assault on the literary lions of the day. Of course, his patron and publisher, Harry Smith, has backed and printed him with peerless courage and style. The book is handsome and—remarkably—inexpensive. As I said: Surprise yourself—and please me—by buying it.

From David Krauso, professor of English, Brown University, January 6, 1981, to Harry Smith:

> Nason's *Dunciad* is a very ambitious and brave work, but since he demolished all the people who might have reviewed it, small wonder then that he has been unfairly ignored. I enjoy reading it in small doses, and return to it often for the fun of it, for the allusion games and put-downs. Not much humor in modern poetry, or blood-letting satire....

The New York City "cold shoulder" and Paul Mariani's *Parnassus* review no doubt effectively undercut what I hoped would become a sizeable audience in the Northeast for my views on current literary corruption. I beg you to understand my interest in rectifying Mariani's slyly conceived disinformation even now more than ten years after the fact. Deconstructing Deconstruction is a daily enterprise. As a further step in this direction, I'd like to quote at length from a long review of *A Modern Dunciad* by the veteran literary commentator Vernon Young. His response coincides almost exactly with my intention in writing the poem and with much else I have stated about such matters. When set against Mariani's contrived dismissal of the *Dunciad,* the contrast may confirm for you — as it does for me — that there has indeed been a very real concerted effort to block the circulation of alternative literary realities. It also provides some evidence that deconstructors of Deconstruction may find it easier to break through to public access on the West Coast than in New York or the East in general. In any event it serves to reinforce our expectation that the future will provide a way around this deadly form of indirect censorship. In *The Western Humanities Review,* autumn, 1979, issue, Vernon Young, then at the State University of New York, Binghamton, wrote:

> Before ending with a look at Richard Hugo — an ending I've contemplated from the beginning — I'd like to mention and recommend an unusual book by Richard Nason titled *A Modern Dunciad* (The Smith, distributed by Horizon Press, $4.00). Written in rhyming couplets after the manner of Pope, Nason's book is precisely what its title announces, a modern version of Pope's *The Dunciad.* In *The Dunciad,* Pope had the Goddess Dullness crown Colley Cibber as her laureate. In Nason's poem, the Goddess Dullness (with her helpmates Anality, Smugness, Self-Service and Sadism) crowns John Ashbery as her King and Laureate. What a wonderful choice! Even if it weren't as well written as it is, and weren't as hilariously funny as it is, I'd recommend this book to all my friends for its central thesis that Ashbery is the King of Dullness. As Nason points out in one of his copious footnotes, dullness in Pope's time was "much more than mere tedium or lack of brilliance. It stood for an aggressive tastelessness, a bumptious grossness that bored, offended and demeaned at one and the same time." Ashbery has always struck me as so much air soufflé, and this description suits him to a T.
>
> Nason's imitation of Pope's manner is nearly perfect in places, and like Pope he combines satire with a serious criticism of the aesthetics and style of much contemporary poetry. He strikes me as off base when he lumps Robert Bly, Galway Kinnell, Joyce Carol Oates and others in with Ashbery. This is a lapse which is unfair to these poets, whose work, even if it can be criticized and satirized on other bases, is surely antithetical to Ashbery's. Still, one good feature of this book is that there's something in it to offend everyone — poets of all schools, academics, minority groups, editors, critics, trade press people and small press people. Nason doesn't pull any punches, and some of the insults are scatological indeed. That's just what makes it so much fun. It's precisely what we need in the small world of poetry, which, as Nason shows, is often quite small, petty, and ass-kissing. To a great extent the book is a social satire, especially when it deals with the collaboration of professors and critics to elevate Ashbery to his current position of eminence. Thus, Harold Bloom becomes a central figure, teetering in his tux on the parapet of Belvedere Castle in Central Park and spouting inanities during the wonderful scene of the games and festivals after Ashbery's crowning at the poem's end.
>
> The book is marvelously quotable; I feel limited only by the necessity to bring this review to a close. Here are some passages:

The Females tear the shroud by Sappho woven
To bloody shreds and ribbons for their coven,
And then employ with Jong her verbal blender
To prove that crap can come from any gender!
There go the tankas, haikus, quickee! Lookie!
They've harnessed Einstein in a Fortune Cookie!
See Dullness now become Mercutio's Mab,
Although a little stoned from sipping Tab:
She's moved so many presses underground,
That vacancies above now quite abound,
And Alternate Composers cough such phlegm,
The world awaits Alternatives to them!

Young also quotes 18 lines from a section I've cited earlier (see Chapter VI) where Dullness steps down the "A"'s in the alphabet until she comes to "Ashbery, John."

> At the end, in the celebration after Ashbery's crowning, W. S. Merwin is chased like a fox through Central Park by Alfred Knopf and Random House; Leonard Randolph from the National Endowment for the Arts runs over a few poets with a government Jeep; Ashbery wins a baking contest in which Donald Justice "took defeat with solemn air,/ Both held and ate his cake, a perfect square"; and Harold declaims from his parapet, "While Ginsberg and the crowd from Old Naropa/ Brought hands to face in holy 'ropa-dopa'!" (Nason's footnote explains that the Buddhist hands-to-face prayer resembles Mohammed Ali's defensive non-boxing, which he calls "ropa-dope.")
>
> The book is 114 pages long and handsomely printed, a bargain for four dollars.
>
> One thing Nason exaggerates I think is Ashbery's influence. He talks about undergraduates scribbling away like miniature Ashberys across the country. But my own experience is that Ashbery's influence wanes outside of New York and New Haven.

So as we see, there seems to be a great deal of actual and potential pressure out there to put Neo-Existential poetry out of business. Hardly a week goes by that new evidence of this emerging countermovement does not find its way to my battered mailbox. The trouble is, as part of its nationally concerted strategy the establishment keeps the main literary outlets bottled up. I foresaw this in the Epilogue to my *Dunciad,* where the Goddess gives King John (Ashbery) advice on how best to monopolize literary expression as a prelude to blowing up the world:

> It's best when all the world is turning dumb
> To follow simple, handy rules of thumb —
> In driving Mankind down the path of hell,

To reassure him all is going well,
That hell is just a home away from home,
Your verse another kind of harmless poem —
Just void his mind while filling up his ear,
Like Muzak while he's in the dentist's chair —
We must not interrupt the media noise,
Nor tolerate the kind of counterpoise
That poets offered once in brash defiance
To all my arts of money, war and science —
Through you we *automate* the rule of Dunce:
Usurp the poet's role, pre-empt response,
Tie-up the presses, satisfy the set,
Relax the prey, and *then* we drop the net!

Not even the new poetry establishment itself would deny that over the last decade it has managed to consolidate its nearly complete monopoly on the publication of poetry and criticism in books and periodicals. The fact that scores of would-be dissidents are aware of this and deplore it has not as yet worked to improve matters much. Among those who have most recently called our attention to this frustrating condition is Robert Peters, a West Coast professor of poetry and a persistent satirist of the new establishment. A tearsheet from the *Small Press Review* arrived in late 1990 wherein Peters repeats the frequent complaint: ". . . there are almost no outlets for alternative voices."

By the way, I do not mention these personal contacts with the growing countermovement to present myself in any way as a literary figure who would care to compete with the celebrity of our Neo-Existential luminaries like Ashbery and Mariani. Except for the denial of money from grants, fellowships and profitable public appearances, anonymity in literary matters is a blessing in disguise. I find my own ever so slight trace of literary recognition a nagging distraction. Mentioning such contacts does, however, serve to provide firsthand evidence of a growing opposition to what is taking place in poetry today. It also serves the secondary purpose of correcting the false impression that poet-critics like Mariani would give of those who oppose them when he writes that "Nason is savaging himself, actively courting defeat, as if he meant to go out in a fiery but meaningless blaze of glory. . . ." On the contrary, I find my formal or traditional literary stance today more congenial and more staunchly supported than ten years ago when Mariani wrote.

The antithesis to Mariani and his kind is beginning to take many new mainstream forms. For example, Bruce Bawer, a poet and critic, again in the pages of *The New Criterion* (November, 1990, issue) in a piece entitled "Formal Poetry in the Land of the Free," approaches the entire question of the Neo-Existential monopoly from a constructive historical point-of-view when he writes:

> ...if poetic revolution was once a cyclical affair—a recurrent, generation-by-generation process of self-renewal—modernism's [read Neo-Existential's] rejection of meter, though revitalizing in the short term proved eventually to be destructive, the beginning of a downward spiral in which each new generation of poets [from Stevens to Ashbery to Simic, let me add] would revolt against its predecessors not by energizing the language of verse but by moving progressively further from the rigors of traditional form and meter, and writing poems that were ever more slack and shapeless.
>   ... What makes this confusion possible, of course, is that these students live in an age when poetry *does* look upon itself as being in a permanent state of revolution, and when the headquarters of that revolution, furthermore, have long since been relocated to the academy; paradoxical though this alliance of academy and poetic revolution may be, even the brightest of teenagers today have never known any other set of circumstances, and so it is difficult for them to see, as Eliot did, that such an alliance is destined to foster a poetry establishment dominated by inert, insular, and technically inept rebels without a cause—a poetry establishment which, for all its stagnancy and need for revitalization, is ironically all the more difficult to overthrow than previous establishments precisely *because* it has taken possession of the very idea of revolution.

But those who appear to be the most aggrieved by the loss of form and substance in current poetry are not writers at all. They are nonliterary persons who regard the appearance of all this minimalist and painterly verse as a sharp falling-off in the quality of American life. One major function of poetry up until recently has been to chronicle the particulars of our immediate history, both as individuals and as a nation. The major effect of deconstructed critical and poetic forms is to eliminate our own history from the inheritance of the generations that come after us. The letters and calls I regularly receive give voice to a profound sense of loss in this respect.

In all this palaver about old and new poetry we have forgotten the main character in this unreal drama—the reader! In all this precious talk about how to teach and how to write poetry most of the new practitioners have failed to note in their critiques that the audience for poetry had all but disappeared outside the university. As monks of a sort, of course, they do not really seem to care. Why should they? Their every need has been provided for within the college system. But what of the once comparatively vast public audience for poetry? Should we conclude that they experience their current deprivation without a sense of being somehow diminished?

The aforementioned Bruce Bawer at the end of his piece (in *The New Criterion*) shifts the focus of his concern from the poet's confusion over free versus structured verse to the unfulfilled needs of the poetry audience itself. He presses into service the argument of Timothy Steele's brand-new *Missing Measures: Modern Poetry and the Revolt against Meter:*

> . . . And it should be emphasized that Steele is not proposing that free verse be abolished; he is merely demonstrating that form and meter are valuable tools which have served the aims of poetry well for millennia, and that these tools are inadequately appreciated by many poets. To be sure, there are doubtless many free-verse poets who, regarding poetry mainly as a means of self-expression, are in the habit of identifying the poem with the self it expresses, and consequently are inclined to see arguments for the value of form and meter as a hostile act against the free-verse poet's self—an attempt to confine, to stifle. Steele, in the final words of his book, implicitly addresses this contemporary poetic emphasis on the poet, and on the ephemeral gratifications of tossed-off, undisciplined verse, by shifting emphasis to the reader, and to the deeper, long-term pleasures that memorable, well-crafted poetry can provide. "Only the poetry of our time," he writes, "can offer the prospect that, after we and those we love have returned to dust, some reader somewhere will be moved by lines that bear witness to us and will commit our words to heart and mind that we may live again." These words strike at the essence of what poetry is, or should be, all about, and in their passion, seriousness, cadence, and amplitude epitomize the very qualities that are most wanting in contemporary free verse.

Vernon Young was not the only reviewer to state that he thought I overestimated Ashbery's importance and influence in all this. Others have said that Harold Bloom's influence has also been overstated. On the contrary, watching developments over the last twenty years has convinced me that the destructive impact upon our literature in general of Bloom and Ashbery has not yet been adequately assessed or fully appreciated. Even so, Bawer's piece is again helpful here. It tells how he reluctantly broke down and finally accepted a job to teach a short-term workshop at "a private high school in New England." He writes as if astounded by the degree to which poetry had been

Bloomiated and Ashberyized (if you will permit me these clumsy coinages) in the secondary school system. After his stay at the school, Bawer summarizes:

> . . . More often, students are encouraged to view Poetry not as an art but as a profession; encouraged not to aspire to excellence but to tailor their work to a marketplace that exalts blandness and mediocrity; encouraged not to work hard at poems over a substantial period of time, but to churn them out like assembly-line products. Moreover, as the poet David Dooley observes in his recent essay "The Contemporary Workshop Aesthetic" (*The Hudson Review,* summer, 1990) workshops tend to produce students who write pretty much the way their teachers do—which means, at least nine times out of ten, that they manufacture tame, slack, and highly derivative free-verse lyrics consisting mostly of (a) jejune personal confession that the poet had made little attempt to render interesting or meaningful, and by means of which he advertises his sincerity and sensitivity; (b) familiar surreal imagery whose intended attraction is presumably its quality of freshness, surprise and subversiveness; and/or (c) lackluster, undiscriminating descriptions of foliage, land forms, and such, the point of which is to demonstrate the poet's responsiveness to nature and his attention to detail.

The above represents a brief but complete inventory of the subject-matter of Ashbery's poetry. The works of Ashbery and Bloom have become the standard instrumentalitics for dismantling all criticism and poetry within our national university system. How could their destructive impact be exaggerated? Bruce Bawer during his brief sojourn in the New England poetry workshop found the wreckage dismaying. Here again he uses the new book by Timothy Steele to extend his own investigation:

> Steele . . . knows that poetry has, in large part, fallen into the hands of anti-intellectuals who have little interest in literary history and who, as he puts it, "confuse what is extrinsic to poetic structure with what is intrinsic to it," reducing "formal poet" (if they acknowledge such a concept at all) to a mere subcategory along with all sorts of artistically meaningless groupings based on politics ("feminist poet") or ethnic background ("black poet"), or sexual orientation ("gay poet"), and defending the most confused and undisciplined free verse by saying that "we should write in a crazy fashion because our times are crazy" [what I have termed in Chapter VI "the scientistic fallacy"]. As Steele observes, such poets don't realize that all times feel crazy to those who live in them, or that by expressing in their poetry a glibly nihilistic philosophy they may "be inviting us to collaborate with the very forces we should resist."

Can we survey the wide destruction within the teaching and writing
of literature today and still conceivably overestimate the part that
Ashbery's dominance has played in all of this over the last fifteen
years? One person who never plays down his own importance is John
Ashbery himself. Lest we forget, he delivers us at least one new
volume a year, sometimes, it seems, even two. What's more, a poet
friend of mine who spends much of his time at writers' colonies in
various parts of the country, reports that Ashbery these days keeps a
sharp weather eye on the doings of the Nobel Committee in Stock-
holm. The further word is, so do all of Ashbery's friends in key places
within American publishing and the university system. They're bang-
ing all the loud gongs and ringing all the big bells to summon the
Nobel to Ashbery in New York. That's the way they got him every
other grant, award and honor that the United States has to offer. Why
shouldn't it work with the Swedes, they inevitably wonder. In fact, I
am told, John has already evinced sharp disappointment that the
Nobel had so far eluded him.

A Nobel Prize for Ashbery? Could that be possible? Twenty years
ago, I would have said, no. But after tracing his well-engineered rise
to fame and fortune, I'm no longer sure of anything of that nature.
The situation recalls the unseating of Helen Douglas for a United
States Senate seat in 1950. She was one of the most powerful people
in the country. Could anyone as crass and callow as Nixon ever defeat
her? Most people didn't think so. When Nixon finally conned his way
to victory, I was more aghast than I had ever been before, or have
been ever since. I remember blurting out the inconceivable to a friend
of mine, "What if a man like Nixon were ever to become President?"
My friend fell into a fit of laughter, coughing-back, "Good God,
things will never get that bad!" *Never* underestimate the gullibility of
people!

Nor their aptitude for connivance. And remember, Ashbery's first
vocational experience was as a publicist for abstract art. He is an
astute self-promoter. So are his many friends. Ashbery's entire literary
career is the result of a well-orchestrated campaign. Vernon Young,
do not underestimate these people: their ambitions for their fatuous
hero are shameless; their industry boundless and their cunning
endless. They are no doubt at this very instant writing letters and
making phone calls to steer the Nobel process in Ashbery's direction.

Should Ashbery finally win the Nobel Prize, the news would probably be greeted on this side of the Atlantic with the same kind of numbed indifference that attaches today to the whole enterprise of current American poetry. After all, as stated, a major effect of the new establishment controlled by Ashbery, Ammons, Bloom and Vendler is to render poetry an absolute nullity on a national scale.

But this would not be the case on the other side of the Atlantic. England has an understandably and persistently high regard for its own versatile language as a stronger and more durable force in the world than its physical empire ever was. Generally speaking, Britons look upon the new *genre* of deconstructed American poetry as ridiculous. The British do not indulge in perennial cultural adolescence the way Americans do. They tend to ignore or denigrate the poetic output of Ashbery and his school. For instance, a review by Hugo Williams in *The New Statesman,* April, 1982, reflects the predominant British view of America's Post-postmodern literature back then — and right now. Williams's review is a refreshing contrast to the obsequious critiques of our laureate that creep forth on this side of the Atlantic. His contempt for Ashbery's poetry is total. He calls it "greeting card doggerel" resulting from the intellectual chaos of the 1950s as it soaked up the kind of Abstraction that gave rise to drip paintings.

> . . . Instead of a paint-pot with holes, [Ashbery] uses his skull to trickle semi-conscious word-doodles into page-shaped moulds which are then delivered to the back gates of universities for processing.
> . . . It is "abstract" in the sense of having been drawn or separated from itself, as in taxidermy, leaving a body of work of which everything and nothing is true. This is great. It allows the real creative work to be done by critics. . . . It's a chance for every student and reviewer to become creative artists: they can even write/roll their own. Go ahead. But imagine at the same time the struggle of John Clare in his asylum seeking lucidity in his madness, then the exact opposite: our tongue-in-cheek hipster playing the cross-eyed loon to academics tremulous of tenure. It isn't a pretty thought.
> Ashbery once said he liked to flick through a book, reading here and there before re-shelving it. His own book finds its way back to the shelf as if by magic. But it isn't the abstraction or abstractness of Ashbery's work that causes it to slip so early from the hands: lots of poets have explored the shape of their thought processes. . . . It is the sheer lack of distinction of those shapes, their predictability, their repetitiveness, and above all the disappointing transparency of his non-sequiturs. . . .
> Ashbery knows it isn't cool to sound like an overgrown hippie any more. . . . Despite the dignifying of his veneers he can never wipe out

the suspicion of a "Hey, man..." at the beginning of every sentence....

What you also hear throughout *Shadow Train* is Ashbery's determination ... to sound serious and grown-up. His achievement is the purging from Sixties underground verse of its only virtue, a certain free-wheeling sense of humor.

... There's a theory that Ashbery is a kind of literary Steinberg, drawing hands drawing themselves out of existence; but I don't see how the visual parallel can be applied here: poetry has no alternative interest to offer, being its own only means of expression. And if you talk about music [Ashbery regards his poetry as the exemplification of both modern painting *and* music; see footnotes to my own *Modern Dunciad*], the music of thought is exactly what sense is: none of that here either. I suppose it's Ashbery's strategy to be without a strategy, to rely on tactics and his cauliflower ear for English. What must he himself make of his extraordinary reputation?

But the battle between Tradition and Deconstruction will be decided in the United States. And it is being hotly contested right now. The ground where American literary culture is being dissolved — and where it must be finally restored — has been staked out in the debate between Cynthia Ozick in *The New Yorker* and Hilton Kramer in *The New Criterion*. We have already shown in Chapter V how these two paced off for a duel over Eliot's anti–Semitism. Ozick finds it sufficient grounds for repudiating "Eliot the man" while somehow preserving a respect for his work as at least retaining some museum value. Kramer, on the other hand, finds her reduction of Eliot both as a person and a poet a kind of gratuitous desecration, like a wad of gum deposited under the armpit of the *Pietà*.

I would go far beyond Kramer's objections. Ozick's *New Yorker* piece appears to be nothing more than a profit-minded sop — or a bucket of slops — for that magazine's aging yuppie readership. In the tens of thousands of words she has written, there is only one mildly interesting section on the degree of conscious strategy Eliot applied to the advancement of his own literary career. And this is a paraphrase of recent biographies. Most of what Ozick has written has the thick, viscous sensational appeal of a confession of what amounts to her adolescent crush on Eliot that now must tearfully give way to more adult considerations — like the great prestige and high price-tag attaching to such a long article in such a high-paying magazine. Both Cynthia Ozick and Helen Vendler should serve as cautionary reminders of the dangers in allowing either one's own teenage infatuations or an inordinate lust for superstar status and money to enter into literary judgments, both early and late.

Ozick goes to great lengths to muffle and disguise her defection from the ranks of traditional criticism. Twist, weep and turn as she might, however, she keeps coming back to the Deconstructionist stance. But this, too, after more than twenty years, seems to have become an aging posture. It may turn out that Ozick is mounting the Deconstructionist bandwagon just as it's grinding to a halt. And when Ozick joins the mobs now rampaging through our university English departments shouting that Deconstruction is somehow more "democratic" than the "elitism" of High Art exemplified by Eliot and the modernistic establishment, she may not only be shamelessly derivative but completely wrong in the bargain. "Eliot condemned the optimism of Democratic American meliorism," she seems relieved to inform us, and "went on to define civilization while omitting some of its highest Western manifestations: the principles of democracy, tolerance and individualism...."

But Deconstruction with its big-booted brutality seems a greater antidemocratic force than Eliot's religious bent ever was. Ozick is preaching to the already-converted when she warns us against anti-Semitism and fascism. As Hilton Kramer points out, by joining in the minimization of even "Eliot the man," Ozick is trivializing the great modernist literary period that finally laid fascism to rest in a grave as broad as the great globe itself. And let me add that Eliot personally, despite his eccentric demurrers over Anglicanism, Classicism and Royalism, was at the active center of that fight against fascism. He repeatedly tried to enlist in both the British and American armed forces. Rejected for an active role, he insisted upon service as a London air raid warden at the height of the German bombardment.

But all of this, too, is far beside the point. I am personally convinced that great literary figures like T. S. Eliot and their heroic sacrifice in their poetry to preserve civilization's highest cultural values and the finest qualities in human experience remain our greatest inspiration in the fight against all forms of human bestiality including fascism. Kramer's response construes Ozick's seeming passivity over the Deconstruction of Eliot and his period as an awful kind of self-induced helplessness. Kramer responds resoundingly:

> "The etiolation of high art seems to me a major loss," she writes, as if so momentous an event could be considered foregone and she, as a writer, had no role to play in its resolution. "High art is dead,"

she writes without question or protest. "The passion for inheritance is dead. Tradition is equated with obscurantism. The wall that divided serious high culture from the popular arts is breached: anything can count as 'text.'" And again: "music is not wanted, history is not wanted, idea is not wanted. Even literature is not much wanted," she writes, as if she were reporting on the course of a civilization other than her own. . . .

With so much sacrificed, Ozick is anxious to insist upon her tightly clenched conviction that Deconstruction presents us with important gains in the way of wider democracy, an improved pluralism or a stronger populism; in short, that Neo-Existential poetry offers a richer soil for a more deeply rooted "nativistic" Americanism as against Eliot's and modernism's "Eurocentrism." But the new group of critics deconstructing Deconstruction like Bruce Bawer and Anthony Steele—let's begin calling them Reconstructionists—have now aggressively begun to question even this. In his "Formal Poetry in the Land of the Free," quoting Steele again, Bawer writes:

> Of course, creative-writing teachers [and Ozick, we might now add] today can dismiss Eliot's objections to the institutionalization of free verse as the grumblings of an elitist snob, a man from St. Louis who turned himself into an Englishman [a "fake Englishman," Ozick calls him]; the great appeal of free verse, for many of them, is that they view it as inherently American, and meter and form as British. . . . Steele rightly criticizes this schematic view, arguing that "meter has nothing in particular to do with . . . England," being "common to the poetries of many different societies [going] back to prehistoric times," and that it is similarly wrongheaded to "talk of an 'American' tradition in poetry, as if this were a single massive flood upon which every poet in our country is obliged to launch his bark." Besides, as Steele points out, even W. C. Williams, in his later years, was displeased by younger poets' absolute renunciation of form and meter, complaining, "Without measure we are lost. But we have lost even the ability to count."
>
> As for the absurd but widespread notion that free verse is somehow democratic and traditional form and meter elitist, Steele advises that those who hold this view should keep in mind that Pound and Wyndham Lewis were Nazi apologists. He observes, too, that "throughout most of literary history, readers have loved and venerated verse more" than prose, and that "its primacy had derived from meter"—which, given the fact that the rise of free verse had seen poetry lose its general audience, makes it seem more reasonable to identify free verse as elitist and metered verse as democratic than to do the reverse. . . .

Now that Deconstruction has overflowed its original source in college English departments and flooded through all the other humanities, more and more Reconstructionist news stories have begun to appear in the daily press. Among these, late in 1990, Richard Bernstein, in *The New York Times,* beneath a banner headline, "The Rising Hegemony of the Politically Correct," began his piece:

> Instead of writing about literary classics and other topics, as they have in the past, freshmen at the University of Texas next fall will base their compositions on a packet of essays on discrimination, affirmative action and civil rights cases. The new program, called "Writing on Difference," was voted in by the faculty last month and has been praised by many professors for giving the curriculum more relevance to real-life concerns. . . .
>
>   . . . The term "politically correct," with its suggestion of Stalinist orthodoxy . . . is being heard more and more across the country in debates over what should be taught at the universities. . . . [T]here is a large body of belief in academia and elsewhere, that a cluster of opinions about race, ecology, feminism, culture and foreign policy defines a kind of "correct" attitude toward the problems of the world, a sort of unofficial ideology of the university. . . .

The increasing frequency of stories like this in the popular press will no doubt hasten public disenchantment with Deconstruction and its various works on the nation's campuses. But dislodging it from its position of academic domination will turn out to be much more difficult. For Deconstruction underwrites its own permanency by making itself a condition of advancement and tenure. There will no doubt be many, many books on this sorry development before any large cracks in Deconstruction begin to signify its ultimate doom. This is one of the themes of Roger Kimball's *Tenured Radicals:* that Deconstructionists, like Neo-Existential poets, ensure their own perpetuity by cleverly outmaneuvering the Reconstructionists.

Kimball documents the chaos within *all* the humanistic disciplines due to the ravages of Deconstruction over the last ten years. But *Tenured Radicals* is most revealing when it chronicles the bizarre events taking place today in the teaching and practice of Deconstructed architecture. Deconstructed literature may cause a certain amount of astonishment and confusion. But, after all, the disfigurement of language is only ideational. It does not cause in most people aesthetic nausea and physical pain. But Deconstructed architecture conceived — and actually built! — to produce aesthetic revulsion and physical discomfort because such conditions characterize the post–Holocaust era we live in [a variation of "the scientist fallacy"] — well, that's another matter altogether.

At one point, Kimball quotes Peter Eisenman. He is a leading architect, we are told, and thought to be a spellbinder at the university lectern. You have to read his words on the page to believe the degree of verbal derangement that Deconstruction has brought about in areas other than the literary. Deconstruction, for example, seems to have turned traditional architecture's sliderules and rulers into so much slapstick rubber being wielded by a bunch of characters who all resemble Groucho Marx. But they're dead serious. Bloom started it all. But Eisenman, coming later, is more "belated," and so must speak (read, "misspeak") more strongly (read, "more crazily"). Kimball quotes Eisenman describing his "Houses III and IV":

> An alternative process of making occupiable form, . . . a process specifically developed to operate as freely as possible from functional considerations. From a traditional point of view, several columns "intrude on" and "disrupt" the living and dining areas as a result of this process. . . . Nonetheless, these dislocations . . . have, according to the occupants of the house, changed the dining experience in a real and more importantly, unpredictable fashion.

This guy makes Harold Bloom sound like a stickler for simple declarative sentences by comparison. Kimball comments on all this with an implausibly straight face. "Please note," he soberly advises us,

> that Eisenman does not assert that the occupants claim that his ill-placed columns have done anything to make "the dining experience" more *pleasant*. Nor would he want them to. For one of the main goals of Eisenman's architecture (and his writing, too, one suspects) is to subvert anything so bourgeois as comfort or intelligibility. As he puts it, his houses "attempt to have little to do with the traditional existing metaphysic of the house, the physical and psychological gratification associated with the traditional form of the house, . . . in order to initiate a search for those possibilities of dwelling that may have been repressed by the metaphysic."

This guy's a real find. He's like a cartoon strip. I could read him forever. Earlier Eisenman's quoted as stating, "this work is an attempt to transcend our traditional view. . . . [I]t is an attempt to alienate the individual from the known way in which he perceives and understand [sic] his environment. . . ." This prompted Kimball, who finally seemed to be getting into the swing of it, to respond

> But the notes are nothing compared to Eisenman's essay. Grandly informing us that "the essence of the act of architecture is the dislocation

of an ever-reconstituting metaphysic of architecture," Eisenman tells us that the six houses that form the subject of his book are all "governed by the intent to define the act of architecture as the dislocation of consequent reconstitution of an ever-accruing metaphysic of architecture." What, you ask, is "an ever-accruing metaphysic of architecture"? Eisenman never says, but it is clear that he has a special liking for the word metaphysic.

And I might add, when he wants to say something else, anything else, it seems, he simply shortens metaphysic to *physic,* causing even Kimball to crack a stuffy smile. . .

Attacks on Deconstruction are beginning to appear in many pivotal places these days. Flip through recent book reviews as I'm doing. Here's an attempt at reconstructing the modern American novel from *The New York Times Book Review,* titled *The Post-Modern Era: The Act of Fiction in an Age of Inflation,* written by Charles Newman with a Preface by our old friend Gerald Graff (see Chapter IV). Reviewer Eric Gould writes:

> By "Formalism" [Newman] means the postmodernist urge to make the subject matter of fiction the nature of fiction itself. Writing becomes a continuous exploration of the conditions of writing. . . .

Let's cut this short simply to note that the prose *genres* in Deconstruction arc suffering from the same kind of solipsism as the poetic forms. And are also the objects of increasing attack from Reconstructionists.

We should also note that as the countermovement intensifies, Harold Bloom removes himself from the spreading fire. You may wish to recall that in Chapter I, foreseeing this development, I wrote:

> By the time the future penetrates the armament of Bloom's thick-mailed, Teutonic argument to the soft, white, freckled personal motives that puff beneath the metal garment, Bloom will have moved to new ground. Anticipating the mounting tempo of the attacks upon his Theory, in order to maintain his "priority," or dominance [or novelty], he will become his own severest critic. . . .

I should have written, "Deconstruction's severest critic. . . ." For, in fact, that's what Bloom's doing these days. Now that Deconstructionists have taken over the university system and his once radical theories have become the norm, Bloom goes beyond simply abandoning them to outright attack. After almost singlehandedly creating such turmoil, he seems to have deserted mainstream literature altogether and turned to writing books about the Bible. Richard Bernstein, in an

interview with Bloom in *The New York Times,* October 24, 1990, on the
occasion of the publication of *The Book of J,* wherein Bloom contends
that large portions of the Hebrew Bible were written by a woman,
describes what can be regarded by old Bloom-watchers as a complete
reversal of form by the arch–Deconstructionist:

> Bloom . . . has . . . warred . . . against . . . deconstruction, the new
> historicism, feminism and Marxist schools. . . . They are not, [Bloom]
> contends, involved in scholarship at all but merely pressing their own
> political causes. . . .

He should know! Reporter Bernstein exhibits himself as a naïve
latecomer to the Bloomian battlefield. In stating that Bloom now wars
against Deconstruction, would it not be journalistically germane to
point out that Bloom is — or was — the primal force in promulgating,
along with Hartman and de Man, Deconstruction in the first place?
And then go on to ascertain, in Bloom's own words, what prompts him
now to attack his own creation?

But Deconstruction swept upon the field without any acceptable ex-
planation as to why it was there in the first place. And those legions
of pathetic New Critics or modernist commentators systematically
destroyed by Bloom and his Deconstruction never so much as emitted
an "ouch!" in the way of pain or protest. So is it any wonder that now,
twenty-five years later, Deconstruction could begin to disappear without a grace note of thanks to the literary world for its self-sacrificial
hospitality? And that Bloom himself, our great, high-booted literary
swashbuckler, can now remove himself from the swirling scene of literary Deconstruction to the tranquil grazing-grounds of hermeneutical exegesis without even touching his lips in the way of "Adieu"!

I don't think that mainstream literature will be bothered by Bloom
again. He has the whole new field of religious literature to conquer.
And many new speeches and interviews to give. After all, the docile
annotators in religious scholarship are not onto him yet. But Bernstein
reports in the same interview, they're beginning to get the message.
"Now Bloom is embroiled in a new controversy," the interviewer
reports; ". . . biblical and other scholars . . . say, among other things,
that he does not know enough about the Bible to be reliable as an inter-
preter of it. . . ." Don't kid yourself, guys, that won't stop him!

This is as good a time as any to say "Goodbye to all this." And to
give thanks that we have survived the awful siege of Deconstruction
in criticism and Neo-Existentialism in poetry. Let's all now pray that

these bizarre literary movements will soon disappear altogether into the all-devouring maw that claimed earlier historical embarrassments like sophism, scholasticism, and the more recent fundamentalist creation theory. And that soon we'll have the further good fortune to witness the return of poetics to its central place in society as the repository of such redemptive sentiments as history, ethics and spirituality.

A Bibliographic Postscript.

Harold Bloom's criticism can be comprehended only as a misdirected and ultimately unavailing search for dogma. He demonstrates overall an obsession with the perverse notion that "all religion is spilled poetry." He states this unmistakably in *Kabbalah and Criticism* (page 52): "Let us say (following Vico) that all religion is apotropaic litany against the dangers of nature, and so is all poetry an apotropaic litany, warding off, defending against death. From our perspective, religion is spilled poetry."

It is at this one point that Bloom attains his singularity, not through any presumed greatness of "strength" on his part, but through a disturbing eccentricity. For if religion is poetry after it is spilled, then poetry before it is spilled is religion as well. It is this misnaming of things that leads at last to the kind of total reductionism that characterizes Bloom's work. He cannot find what he is looking for because what he is looking for is not there in the first place.

So he can only conclude, as he does, "Alas, a poem *has* nothing, and *creates* nothing" (*Kabbalah and Criticism*, page 122). From this it is simple to proceed, as he does, to the premise that anything can be a poem. And the nearest substitute for a poem, in Bloom's aesthetic, is one's own sense of what lies immediately outside the poem, or "between texts," as he would put it. And this sense is plainly and simply a sense of your own self. So your reaction to the poem, your criticism of it, becomes the poem.

Obviously anything is possible within such a world. It is a world without referents or verifiable properties. Insofar as it is shared by Neo-Existential poets, it is most readily comprehended as comedic, as a kind of unintended slapstick. But in Bloom it is ponderously appointed with religious dogma and litany. Or, as it finally works, it is a futile attempt to substitute poetry for the beatific effects of dogma and litany in religion.

So Bloom's search for these things finally reduces all poetry to a search for the sublime. He then discards even these surviving sublime fragments as insufficient to the demands of his own appetites for the dogmatic absolute in poetry. Bloom insists he is not a Kabbalist. But his tone throughout until he absorbs the Kabbalah is that of a disillusioned dogmatist. He also says he is not ıstructionist. But the result of his work is the dismantling of the entire structure of Western Literature to make room for his own pervasive presence as criticism personified.

When compared to his own spiritual expectations, while poets may be "heroic" in their aspirations, they are in fact invariably mean and abject in their attainment of the sublime and must be upended or amended. So in his practice Bloom finds *all* poets still trapped in some corner of themselves, of nature or of death, or some composite of all three. The human ego, the nature of the world and the death of all things are the inevitable conditions of human existence itself. How can Bloom deny poetry because it succumbs to such conditions?

What drives Bloom to undertake a seemingly insane plunge beyond this common sense of reality? Long after Deconstruction itself has gone aglimmering, though Bloom may still be among us in other fields, the one important book about Bloom may be finally written. It will focus upon his days at Yale in the Sixties and how these reflected and exacerbated the awful psychic deprivations that must have been inflicted upon him in his childhood. Such a book could finally explain just why and how Bloom was driven to exercise his over-compensating Oedipal drives to overwhelm literary tradition as a means of achieving domination over his critical colleagues at Yale.

Boiled Grass and the Broth of Shoes makes only indecisive gestures in this direction. The motivating forces in Bloom's career remain unexplored. Deconstruction itself is so chimerical, so *unreal* that no real effort is needed to discover the actual motives of those who propagated it. Those we finally call Reconstructionists are urged on by a hard sense of reality reasserting itself. They would stand before the task of constructing an antithesis to Bloom and his Theory as I did, unnerved by the prospect that before horseshit could be piled high enough to offset it, the towering pile that is Bloomian Deconstruction would have toppled of its own weight. Common sense and inertia work against such an undertaking.

It is enough to remember that Bloom's search for dogma takes place on "a *point* of the primordial, where presence and absence [of God, reality, human existence] co-exist by continuous interplay" (*Kabbalah and Criticism*, p. 53). Anything can happen at that "primordial point." And it usually does. Bloom can get rid of Derrida's wandering "trace," turn the pyramid of tradition upside-down with poets on the bottom at the pinnacle, or put himself as the critic on the broad base at the top. Upon this fantastical "primordial point" where "presence and absence [everything and nothing] co-exist by continous interplay," Bloom, his Theory, his case and his career — and his Deconstruction — must finally rest. Nowhere!

By the time you find "the primoridal point," Bloom will be gone. As in fact he has already departed for the field of religious studies, where his search for dogma will not be cluttered by poetic distractions. Thank god for that. Yes, he's already raised some hell in hermeneutics with his *The Book of J* (1990), where he tries to capitalize on the feminist audience left untapped in his Deconstructionist enterprise. Just follow the goldbrick road to the primordial point.

Books by Bloom and Others

Bloom, Harold. *The Visionary Company: A Reading of English Romantic Poetry.* Ithaca, N.Y.: Cornell University Press, 1961 (enlarged and revised edition, 1971). This book contains the old, "weak," traditional criticism that Bloom renounces later. Bloom's critiques of the standbys, from Blake to Wordsworth with a dozen other peripheral poets thrown in, are, by his own later lights, somewhat routine, though they do bring into play both ancient and modern commentators who serve as salients in his later Deconstructionist dogma. But the book did not manage to bring him what he craved so desperately at Yale, priority over all of literature, and so over all of his colleagues in the Yale English Department.

Bloom, Harold. *The Ringers in the Tower.* Chicago: University of Chicago Press, 1971. This book, too, remained in the same drab, undistinguished manner. Though it predates *The Anxiety of Influence* by only two years, it might have been two hundred, or two thousand. For Bloom's Theory, as we now know, can blow away epics with its merest exhalation, including his own early work. This book extends that earlier work to Tennyson and Browning and a dozen moderns and postmoderns, including Ginsberg, Geoffrey Hill (in England) and Ashbery and Ammons. But in Bloom's view, it all turns into just so many words on the page, as expendable as used kleenex after *The Anxiety of Influence.* This marks the end of Bloom's struggle to realize "the sublime" based upon an absolute dogma through tradition. He still finds all of his objects of scrutiny, the poets themselves, helplessly trapped in the self, nature and death, Shelley's *cul-de-sac.*

Bloom, Harold. *The Anxiety of Influence: A Theory of Poetry.* New York: Oxford University Press, 1973. Here's the spot where Bloom's "primordial point" becomes his own pivot to hell. It is his own *Mein Kampf,* where he burns the past and freezes the future. This book tropes against his own better nature that accepted the human condition, and his own maxim that underlies his earlier criticism, that man had better accept "less than all" (page 11, *The Ringers in the Tower*). This is the point where Faustus also faced the choice between his own soul and personal omnipotence. Bloom, too, fails the diabolical confrontation and opts for an unyielding ambition that shoulders aside all tradition and earlier learning, the unseemly clutter of the remnants of the New Criticism and the modest early forays into Deconstruction of his colleagues at Yale (Paul DeMan and Geoffrey Hartman) for an unconfined supremacy, in the manner of Macbeth, Faust and some equally unsavory near-contemporaries like Stalin and Hitler. This is where Bloom equates criticism with poetry and then climbs up over it, to make criticism a replacement for poetry and himself a replacement for all other criticism through the "strength" of his "misreading." If you have to ask what's wrong with that, then you will never know. You can join those shadows who believed in alchemy. There are crowds of them in our past, many just like them in our present. Let me repeat here, Deconstruction's main impetus is a drive for power on the part of those who formulated it.

Bloom, Harold. *Kabbalah and Criticism.* New York: Seabury Press, 1975. In this book, Bloom completes his search for religious dogma and litany. He finally locates the dialectical model he needs to energize his stance of personal critical supremacy. The collective Kabbalah constitutes Bloom's Hegel. As for his denial of being a Kabbalist and a Deconstructionist? If it quacks like a duck, it's a duck. He also states that he simply happened upon Kabbalah. That he didn't know his revisionism, its ratios, alienation, belatedness and, most importantly, its anxieties were presaged by it. Bloom says a lot of things. Like the utterances of Faust, his own lexicon from the outset struck me as highly suspect by virtue of his megalomaniacal ambitions. Kabbalah invested Bloom's Theory with the kind of premedieval and therefore exotic trappings that might engage the craving for litany and dogma that postmodern criticism is general exhibited, especially at Yale for some reason that can be part of the book that someone — not I — must write or is writing now.

Bloom, Harold. *A Map of Misreading.* New York: Oxford University Press, 1975. This grounds the premedieval Kabbalah in the present. Here we are presented with a double-action syncretism to work horizontally across all texts or traditions, those known and unknown, real and imagined, and, vertically, up-and-down the poet's consciousness, or unconsciousness to graph and index every conceivable kind of literary experience, except that of common sense and everyday reality. This Map has about as much practical utility or real substance as the key to the flagpole, or the red oil for the red lamp, or the snipe in the snipe hunt they used to send you on during your first summer at camp.

Bloom, Harold. *Figures of Capable Imagination.* New York: Seabury Press, 1976. Here Bloom proceeds to absorb precursors (competitors) into his Dogma of Deconstruction. The emphasis now is upon the moderns and Bloom's own contemporaries such as Ashbery and Ammons. He finds them all still in Shelley's shade, confined in their own self, or in nature or in death. So, through the use of the Map and application of the dialectic of *Anxiety,* he shows them a path to the poems they might have written or, less likely now, the poems they should, could or might yet write to give them strength to attain a firmer sublime beyond their ellipses, indirections, or problematical forms, where they might cross "the boundary between the visual and the visionary." All this of course is about as useful as a laser to open a can of worms. Everything and everybody falls short of history prior to *Anxiety* and the *Map.* How could it be otherwise once all are subjected to the reduction at Bloom's "primordial point," where everything is nothing, and nothing is everything. Duns Scotus again (*Boiled Grass,* page 54 above).

Bloom, Harold. *Poetry and Repression.* New Haven, Conn.: Yale University Press, 1976. Bloom has finally found his spiritual authority. He's regularly published by Yale at last. If the Yale U.P. doesn't prove such authority, his arbitrary tone and autocratic attitudes will. By this book, he has become an overbearing dogmatist who makes Eliot seem a diffident schoolboy by comparison. Bloom now holds sway over all as the "strongest" critic in the history of literature. Here he returns to the great Romantics and absorbs them all through his double-action syncretisms, as so many mice for his python-like appetites. If *The Anxiety of Influence* was his *Mein Kampf,* then *Poetry and Repression* becomes his religious *Summa,* intertwining good and evil into a

Bloomian double-helix. One caution here: In this book Bloom ignores Freud's warning against acting out the unconscious without sublimation. He could say on page 11 in *The Ringers in the Tower* (1971): "The Freudian rationalism, wisely refusing heroic failure, insists that less than all had better content man, for there can be no satisfaction in satisfaction anyway." But by the time of *Poetry and Repression* five years later, like the dictator in his final paranoid phase, Bloom has become brutal and despotic in his apotropaic dogma and litanies. Even in *Kabbalah and Criticism* (1975), he could nod to the real world by admitting, "No one would survive socially if he or she went around assuming or saying that he or she had to be misinterpreted..." (*Kabbalah and Criticism*, page 121). But by the time of *Poetry and Repression* (page 140), Bloom chastises us with the exact opposite: "This late in tradition, we all come to one another smothered in and by meaning: we die daily, facing one another, of our endlessly mutual interpretations and self-interpretations. We deceive ourselves, or are deceived, into thinking that if we could be interpreted rightly, or interpret others rightly, then all would be well. But by now—after Nietzsche, Marx, Freud and their followers and revisionists—surely we secretly—all of us—know better. *We know that we must be misinterpreted in order to bear living, just as we know we must misinterpret others if they are to stay alive, in more than the merely minimal sense. The necessity of misreading one another is the other daily necessity that accompanies sleep and food, or that is as pervasive as light and air...*" (italics added).

So much for Bloom's attempt to move away from the "primordial point" to some objective point in everyday reality. If you followed his advice you'd be thrown swiftly in jail. But this is where Bloom's Deconstruction ends, right where it began in some sort of limbo. He himself, however, is no longer there. He has abandoned the whole business for the fresher, lusher fields of Biblical studies. I hope our scholars this time are braced for what's coming.

Vendler, Helen. *Part of Nature, Part of Us.* Cambridge, Mass.: Harvard University Press, 1980. *The Music of What Happens: Poems, Poets, Critics.* Cambridge, Mass.: Harvard University Press, 1988. Offhand you might infer from the pliability, not to say flimsiness, of her criticism that Vendler would offer American literature some relief from the intimidating dogma of Bloom's work. And superficially this may appear to be the case. Vendler's literary evaluations are always impressionistic and undemanding. They are invariably amiable in their approach to both her subjects and her readers. But watch out—behind her blind at Harvard, Vendler is a tough, disciplined Deconstructionist, holding down the Harvard flank in Bloom's "warfare" against Tradition at Yale. Her dipsy-doodle career owes everything to Bloom's early maneuvers in Deconstruction, which Vendler confirms with the ease and insouciance of a perfect dancing partner. She mimics almost exactly Bloom's revisions of the past. And his elevation of Ashbery and Ammons and a dozen other Neo-Existential poets in the postmodern canon. Behind the scenes, however, on the all-important prize and money panels, Vendler on her own comes down even harder against form and tradition in *all* things literary. Bloom as a presumed force unto himself tends to ignore such extraliterary matters. Not Vendler. On the campus and in the national literary marketplace she is known as a tough operative and just as covetous of her only profit and aggrandizement as Bloom is of his. She, then, is a political animal. The good cop to Bloom's bad.

Gordon, Lyndall, *Eliot's Early Years,* 1977; *Eliot's New Life,* 1988. New York: Farrar, Straus and Giroux. Gordon's direct, nonpolemical approach to biography tends to cut through the confusion and controversy that has worked to becloud Eliot's social and political ideas. This is the clearest and most diligent of Eliot's biographies to date. Gordon's account of Pound's collaboration on *The Waste Land* is both comprehensive *and* specific. It establishes Pound as nothing less than the coauthor of that twentieth-century opus. Still, it leaves us free to speculate upon what kind of confused and indecisive poem *The Waste Land* might have been without Pound. Even whether it would have been published at all. Or had it been published, lacking Pound, would it have become the signature for modernity, which as we learned later, and now are reassured by Gordon was as much (or more) the signature of Pound as of Eliot himself? This leads us finally to wonder what would Modernism have been without Pound? And our own postmodernism? Lyndall Gordon helps us to imagine such things.

Eliot, T.S. *T.S. Eliot, The Waste Land, A Facsimile and Transcript of the Original Drafts Including the Annotations of Ezra Pound,* edited by Valerie Eliot. New York: Harcourt Brace Jovanovich, 1971. Such speculations as Gordon (above) invites haunt the original manuscript, heavily deleted and amended by Ezra Pound's impetuous and yet incisive scribblings. The reappearance of this key manuscript after its prolonged disappearance is a historical saga in and of itself.

Eliot, T.S. *The Complete Poems and Plays 1909–1950.* New York: Harcourt, Brace & World, 1952.

Eliot, T.S. *Selected Essays.* New York: Harcourt Brace Jovanovich, 1978.

Eliot, T.S. *The Letters of T.S. Eliot, Vol. I 1898–1922,* edited by Valerie Eliot. New York: Harcourt Brace Jovanovich, 1988.

Eliot, T.S. *The Use of Poetry & The Use of Criticism. Studies in the Relation of Criticism to Poetry in England.* The Charles Eliot Norton Lectures for 1932–33. Cambridge, Mass.: Harvard University Press, 1986.

Eliot, T.S. *Selected Prose of T.S. Eliot,* edited with an introduction by Frank Kermode. New York: (Harcourt Brace Jovanovich, Publishers); Farrar, Straus and Giroux, 1975.

Pound, Ezra. *The Letters of Ezra Pound 1907–1941,* edited by D.D. Paige. London: Faber and Faber, 1951.

Carpenter, Humphrey. *A Serious Character: The Life of Ezra Pound.* New York: Delta, 1988.

H.D. *End to Torment; A Memoir of Ezra Pound, with the Poems from "Hilda's Book" by Him.* New York: New Directions, 1979.

H.D. *Tribute to Freud.* Foreword by Norman Holmes Pearson. New York: McGraw-Hill, 1974.

H.D. *Selected Poems.* New York: Grove Press, 1957.

Spender, Stephen. *The Thirties and After.* New York: Vintage Books, 1979.

Ashbery, John. *Self-Portrait in a Convex Mirror.* New York: Penguin Books, 1976.

O'Hara, Frank. *The Selected Poems,* edited by Donald Allen. New York: Vintage Books, 1974.

Crane, Hart. *The Complete Poems and Selected Letters and Prose of Hart Crane,* edited with an introduction and notes by Brom Weber. New York: Doubleday/Anchor, 1966.

Kimball, Roger. *Tenured Radicals: How Politics Has Corrupted Our Higher Education.* New York: Harper and Row, 1990.

Nason, Richard. *A Modern Dunciad.* New York: The Smith, 1978.

Nason, Richard. Preface to *Old Soldiers.* New York: The Smith, 1989.

Nason, Richard. Prose introductions to certain poems in *The Ballad of the Dollar Hotel and Other Poems.* Harrisburg, Pa.: Mountain Laurel Publications, 1984.

Newspaper, Periodical and Journal Articles

Some of the newspaper articles and periodical essays listed below have already been cited in the body of the book. Others have not. Many germane articles have been omitted altogether, because of their incidental nature and great number down through the years.

Barton, John. Review of Harold Bloom's *The Book of J* (New York: Grove Weidenfeld) in *The New York Review of Books,* November 22, 1990.

Bernstein, Richard. Interview with Harold Bloom upon the publication of *The Book of J,* in *The New York Times,* October 24, 1990.

Broyard, Anatole. Review of Helen Vendler's *Part of Nature, Part of Us,* in *The New York Times,* March 29, 1980.

Elton, William. "A Glossary of the New Criticism." *Poetry,* December, 1948; January and February, 1949.

Graff, Gerald. "Fear and Trembling at Yale," essay on the "agonies" of anxiety in Deconstruction, in *The American Scholar,* Vol. 46, 1977.

Kramer, Hilton. "The Triumph of Misreading," an essay on Bloom's criticism, in The New York Times Book Review, August 21, 1977.

Mariani, Paul. Review of Richard Nason's *A Modern Dunciad* in *Parnassus: Poetry in Review,* fall-winter, 1982, pp. 265–69.

Materassi, Mario. Interview with Richard Nason; in *La Nazione,* Florence, Italy, May 30, 1981.

Sisson, C.H. Review of Harold Bloom's *Ruin the Sacred Truths* (Cambridge, Mass.: Harvard University Press, 1989) in *The New York Times Book Review,* Sunday, February 26, 1989.

Spears, Monroe. Review of Helen Vendler's *Part of Nature, Part of Us,* in *The Washington Post,* April 6, 1980.

Williams, Hugo. Review of John Ashbery's *Shadow Train* (Carcanet Press), in *The New Satesman* (London), April 2, 1982.

Young, Vernon. Review of Richard Nason's *A Modern Dunciad* in *The Western Humanities Review,* Vol. 33, No. 4, Autumn, 1979.

Reading in Reconstruction

Back in the early 1980s, of course, you could be a Reconstructionist without rallying beneath that banner by name. My own *A Modern Dunciad* was nothing if not Reconstructionist, though as far as I know that word had not yet appeared as the antithesis to "Deconstructionist." I was well into the present work before it became clear that my book was only a small part of a national movement informally massing itself against literary Deconstruction and all of its works.

So, at some point, in late 1989, I suppose, I began to use the word "Reconstructionist." At about the same time, I found a staunch ally for what I was doing in *The New Criterion,* a magazine that has as one of its founding objectives apparently the restoration of literary tradition and form in American literature.

Just as so many doing the work do not call themselves Deconstructionists, those I name below probably do not see themselves as Reconstructionists. Thank god for the small favor of one less label, I guess we should add. Even so, at this early juncture it may be helpful to list recent essays in periodicals to underscore the movement of Reconstruction.

I have cited a few of these in the last chapters of *Boiled Grass.* Certain of them also refer to other books and essays for further collateral reading in what will surely become a major concern throughout the 1990s — and what will likely be called Reconstruction. As dismal as was the sight of Deconstruction leveling all form and tradition at our universities over the last couple of decades, the picture of things falling back together to assume their old traditional shape (with some modifications for postmodernity in the current decade, of course) will be a much jollier one!

Kramer, Hilton. "Cynthia Ozick's Farewell to T.S. Eliot — and High Culture," in *The New Criterion,* February, 1990. This is Kramer's first response to:

Ozick, Cynthia. "T.S. Eliot at 101." *The New Yorker,* November 20, 1989.

Kramer, Hilton. "Cynthia Ozick, T.S. Eliot and High Culture: An Exchange" between Kramer and Ozick," *The New Criterion,* April, 1990.

Kimball, Roger. "Art and Ideas in the Eighties." *The New Criterion,* April, 1990.

Bawer, Bruce. "Formal Poetry in the Land of the Free," *The New Criterion,* November, 1990. In his essay, Bawer makes good use of:

Dooley, David. "The Contemporary Workshop Aesthetic." *The Hudson Review,* summer, 1990, issue. And:

Steele, Timothy. *Missing Measures: Modern Poetry and the Revolt Against Meter.* Fayetteville: University of Arkansas Press, 1990. And:

Bly, Robert. *American Poetry: Wilderness and Domesticity.* New York: Harper and Row, 1990. Reviewed by Bruce Bawer in *The New Criterion,* October, 1990.

Bradbury, Malcolm. Review of *Signs of the Times: Deconstruction and the Fall of Paul DeMan* by David Lehman. (New York: Poseidon Press, 1991), in *The New York Times Book Review,* Sunday, February 24, 1991.

This Postscriptural attempt to bracket Deconstruction and its impending demise should naturally end with a tribute to the thousands of writers who in the last twenty or more years have continued their work in comparative obscurity without any concessions to Deconstruction *or* its handmaiden Neo-Existential poetry.

With this in mind, I would like to salute Thomas McGrath, who died last year (1990) after producing no fewer than a score of books of prose and poetry that by their nature, without announcement, stood in staunch opposition to all academic fads, fashions and trends, which have been, especially in the case of Deconstruction, the very death of American literature.

McGrath, Thomas. *Death Song,* edited by Sam Hamill and posthumously published. Port Townsend, Wash.: Copper Canyon Press, 1991.

A review of *Death Song* by J.P. White in *The New York Times Book Review,* Sunday, March 10, 1991, reminds us that McGrath's opus, "Letter to an Imaginary Friend," was composed between 1962 and 1985. This period saw the ascendency of Deconstruction and Neo-Existential poetry over our entire literary landscape. Yet somehow McGrath persisted in his 329-page epic. White in his review declares McGrath may be finding his long-sought audience at last: "Over the last decade, more and more readers have discovered his beautifully cadenced work. Yet by and large, McGrath has been overlooked by the arbiters of literary taste. Most poets and editors pigeonhole him as a maverick, a political poet or, worse yet, a regionalist. His work—either in its bold and commodious poetic line or in its social implications—has always been viewed as outside the mainstream."

We are now beginning to see that the "mainstream" in American literature after 1965 (and the advent of Bloom and Ashbery) turns out to be as incidental, misleading and trifling as a prefab waterfall in a spiritual theme park. We should perhaps begin our return to the salutary surge of form and tradition by partaking of McGrath's presence in our neglected immediate past history—and so, of course, of his many books of poetry. Let's both finish and begin at once by quoting a little further from White's review of McGrath's work:

"In 'Letter' one finds elements that are missing from most American poetry: an inspection of history from the street, an imagination imbued with facts, an uncanny grasp of the politically absurd, an appetite for mockery and affection and a gift for describing the toils and pleasures of work. In this most readable of epics, history and eternity roll up their shirt sleeves and go to work in the grease of dreams. . . .

". . . McGrath combined a sacramental, pagan view of life with a radical prairie populism rooted in the diversity of the American people and the sweep of the land. Using a controlled yet fluid six-beat line reminiscent of Whitman, McGrath translated personal myth and memory into a stirring account of history and politics as they were experienced on the farms of post–Depression America. In a voice at once public and remarkably private, in 'Letter' he created a new form that might be called historical lyricism—and quite possibly this century's most persuasive and entertaining poem about struggles for broad-based social change."

Index.